Loyal Adolphus Alford

A Trip to the Skies

The Stars! The Stars! Ecce Coelum

Loyal Adolphus Alford

A Trip to the Skies
The Stars! The Stars! Ecce Coelum

ISBN/EAN: 9783337041786

Printed in Europe, USA, Canada, Australia, Japan

Cover: Foto ©ninafisch / pixelio.de

More available books at **www.hansebooks.com**

A Trip to The Skies.

THE STARS! THE STARS!

Ecce Cœlum.

BY

Rev. L. A. ALFORD, D. D., LL. D.,

Honorary member of the Society of Science, Letters and Art, of London, England, and President of the A. A. Association.

LOGANSPORT, IND.

PUBLISHED BY THE AMERICAN ANTHROPOLOGICAL ASSOCIATION, OF LOGANSPORT, IND., U. S. A., AND BY THE SOCIETY OF SCIENCE, LETTERS AND ART, LONDON, ENG.

1884.

DEDICATED TO

LONDON,  LOGANSPORT,

SCIENCE, LETTERS AND ART.

PREFACE.

I have been permitted to read the advance sheets of Dr. L. A. ALFORD's Work, entitled "*A Trip to the Skies.*" It describes an imaginative journey from the Earth to the various orbs of the sky, and the different systems of the universe, which constitute its grand unity, and explains the general principles of astronomy in a popular form. It opens to the mind the immensity of Creation and leads our thoughts to adore and worship its mighty Author. The style is fresh and spirited, and as grand and grave as the subject is; it is very entertaining, as well as instructive, and not without an occasional flash of becoming humor. I have read the advance sheets with much interest and pleasure.

HORACE P. BIDDLE.

The Author of the "Trip to the Skies" would only remark to those abroad, that the Hon. Horace P. Biddle is Chancellor of the American Department of the London (Eng.) Society of Science, Letters and Art"--the Author of a score of popular Works---late Supreme Judge of Indiana, and is the possessor of the largest private or public Library, at his "Island Home," of any in the State.

INTRODUCTION.

BY REV. S. FLEMING, PH. D. LL. D.

The starry firmament, from the earliest ages of human history, has been an object of intense admiration and study. The deep blue vault above us, apparently a vast concave sphere revolving around the earth daily, jetted with twinkling stars of various magnitudes, set in various groups and clusters, have ever attracted the attention of the old and young as surpassing in beauty, any other object of Nature upon which the eye rests, inducing in the minds of different persons questions as varied as their intelligence; from the child query—"How I wonder what you are?" to the profounder questions pertaining to the constitution, relations and mission of these celestial objects which have engaged the thoughts of intelligent minds for many thousands of years.

The sublime panorama moving in stately grandeur from age to age, preserving its order of orbits within orbits, of systems within systems, has not only challenged the admiration of star-gazers, but it has evoked an explanation of the phenomena, has taxed the powers of mathematics to determine the magnitudes, distances, centers of motion and velocties of individual suns and systems, and invited the profoundest men of science and philosophy to explain the cosmogony or science of the genesis of the heavens and the earth, the geology, or constitution of the stars, the attractive force which binds together the universal system, from the infinitesimal meteoric particle which comes flashing down from the apparent voids of space, to the immense aggregates, millions of miles in diameter; to explain the phenomena of the diverse shades of the seven primary colors, from the deep red to the pure violet, and the seven voices of the spheres, pealing forth *eon* to *eon*, "in reason's ear," the anthem of their complex and sublime motions.

> "Forever singing as they shine,
> The hand that made it is Divine."

Astronomy may well claim to have been the most ancient of the sciences. All the nations of antiquity have preserved records of their observations of the celestial bodies. Even the symbols and allegories preserved in their histories, give evidence of the highest antiquity of this science. Thus not only Egyptian and Chaldean shepherds who "watched their flocks by night," in the extended vale of the Nile or on the beautiful plains of Bethlehem, gazed with intelligent interest and intense delight upon the clear blue vault studded with stars of varied glories, but "wise men," Jewish astronomers, wended their way for hundreds of miles from their homes in Persia or Arabia, following the leadings of the "star they had seen in the East," to honor the new-born King, thus honoring the connection of Science and Religion, which should never have been divorced.

But we must travel back in thought, through the ages to the earliest periods of history, to find evidences of the primeval culture of astronomy. The familiar manner in which Job, the oldest writer or the sacred scriptures, refers to Arcturus, Orion and Pleiades, shows that at that period the prominent clusters of stars with their central suns, and the constellations with their orders of motion, were known and named. Still farther back a thousand years, remarkably exact calculations had been made pertaining to the solar system. It is recorded that when Alexander the Great, took Babylon, in the year 331 B. C., his Philosopher, Calisthenes, found in the tower of Babel, which after the "confusion of tongues" had been used for an astronomical observatory, calculations of eclipses for 1903 years preceding, giving evidence that these calculations were made 2234 years B. C., according to the shortest chronology. Further, Chinese records state that in the year 2608 B. C., Hoang Ti, the Emperor, caused an observatory to be built, for the purpose of correcting the calander, and for other objects, and that the year was subsequently determined to consist of $365\frac{1}{4}$ days, nearly the exact period as now found.

The connection of the stars with the destiny of mankind, was suspected at an era nearly coetaneous with the study of the motions of the celestial bodies, and thence gradually Astrology, which in ancient times included both Astronomy proper and the art of foretelling the destinies of men and Empires by the aspect of the stars, became the controlling system of knowledge, cherished by all the nations of antiquity, its influence extending down through the periods of history to the time of Copernicus. Ancient astronomy, therefore, while cultivated for its intrinsic value, and the pleasure it has ever afforded, must be regarded as having been chiefly promoted as the hand-maid of astrology.

After thousands of years, during which pantheism and theism, science and religion, as well as true and false theories of Cosmogony, have been in conflict, the history of mankind brings us to the period of established science, in which we find Christian philosophy taking the symbols of the early and rude ages, and utilizing them for the illustration of the most sublime teachings of Theology. Thanks to the esteemed Author of "*A Trip to the Skies*," for leading reverent and appreciative minds up into celestial excursions in illimitable space, to bask in the "sweet influences of Pleiades," to discover the "bands of Orion," to find "the hidings of the Power that brings forth Mazzaroth (the twelve signs of the Zodiac) in his season," that "guides Acturus and his sons," that "spreads out the North, high over the empty space, and hangs the Earth upon nothing!—thus bringing the thoughts to contemplate the immensity of the universe, and the grandeur of the motions of suns and systems around the central Throne of the Almighty, who upholds "the pillars of the Universe;" and thus by a new, sublime and interesting path, rich with its varied scenery, leading us

"Through Nature, up to Nature's God."

The celestial scenery never becomes old, nor loses its pristine charms. The deepest thinkers and most profound investigators, who have devoted their lives to the study of the stars, have ever had an increasing longing to know more of those sparkling wonders. Very great and rapid has been the progress of astronomy since the determination of the laws of planetary and stellar motion, especially since the introduction of the larger class of telescopes, the invention of the spectrescope and the method of the spectrum analysis by which the character of the luminous rays determine both the elements and distance of bodies. The desire has become increasingly intensified to penetrate the depths of space and solve the problem pertaining to the nebulous phenomena which send down the path of light, from almost infinite distances, evidences of myriads of stellar systems.

But every additional astronomical fact discovered, confirms the accepted doctrine, that the universe—the original conception of which was limited to the phenomena of the revolving firmament—is one all related system of being, generated by one set of forces, and bound together by one system of laws. Hence there can be no isolation, either of a single body, group cluster or nebulæ,—all are related by one system of complex motion, revolving like "wheels within wheels," the smaller systems being subordinate to the larger; thus as the earth is the center of the lunar motion, the two forming a binary system, so the Sun, Vega and Sirius, respectively constitute centers of our solar group, and cluster systems.   *   *   *   *

So it seems quite probable, that Alcyone, chief of the seven stars, is the center of our nebular system, made up of innumerable cluster systems, with unformed nebulous or gaseous matter, and which includes all the stars visible to the naked eye, with myriads of others too distant and comparatively small to be seen without the telescope.

The magnitude of the respective centres above noticed, have been ascertained to be as follows: The Earth's volume is about fifty times that of the Moon; the Sun's volume, 1,252,700 times that of the Earth; Vega more than 300 times that of the Sun; Sirius, 2,000 times larger than the Sun; Alycone, about 12,000 times the volume of the Sun. The distances of these orbs respectively from the Sun are given as follows: Mean distance of the Sun from the Earth, 91,430,000; —of Vega from the Sun about 70 trillions of miles;—of Sirius from the Sun, 125 trillions;—of Alcyone about 3,500 trillions.

The periods of revolution of our Group and Cluster Systems have not been definitely determined, owing to the extreme difficulties of exact observations, especially of the complicated motions of immense numbers of stars which appear in the field of view. Yet the direction and rate of motion of individual stars and groups, called "Star Drifts," have been in many cases approximately calculated—partly by telescopic and partly by spectroscopic observations. Some stars have been found to move at the rate of thirty miles per second. One of the most favorable groups for observation includes five of the stars in Ursa Major, which Prof. Higgins found to be moving in the same general direction at the rate of seventeen miles per second of time, so great and so wonderful is the fleetness of the Stars in the Stellar Skies.*

NOTE.--For further information in reference to the Classification of Sciences, and the general accepted Theory of Cosmogony, the reader is referred to a work published by Dr. Fleming, called PAN DUALISM.

A TRIP TO THE SKIES.

> The living mind stops not its thought,
> At death, but flies beyond;
> It goes not willingly to naught,
> But fain would correspond
> With all the things that never die,
> Throughout the earth or in the sky.
>
> The living soul knows not of death,
> Below, around on high;
> For if it be indeed God's breath,
> He dies if it must die,
> As what God gave, that He will give
> While God exists man's soul will live.
> —*H. P. Biddle.*

CHAPTER I.
THE HEAVENS.

To obtain a general or a comprehensive knowledge of the starry-decked heavens, we must take into consideration a corresponding conception of the heavenly bodies—the vast magnitude of the work of creation.

To do this we must eliminate the most profound conceptions of chaos and matter, of void and spheres; of force and order that the human mind can possibly comprehend.

We must also fully understand that LIFE FORCE

is the only exhaustless force in the universe, and that Deity alone possesses this unlimited life force. That attractions and projections are his creations as much as worlds, or systems of worlds.

To think that this earth, when in comparison with the Solar Sun, is like to a cherry stone associated with a ball two feet in diameter, and then to know, that this great, bright sun in our heavens, when in association with other suns in other systems, is as inferior to them as our earth is to him—to know this and to launch out into a partial survey of such unlimited majesty and splendor demands more than an ordinary comprehension, for astronomy embraces the heavens universal. What is this immense Universe? And does this vast machine move itself, govern itself, regulate itself?

Dare we look up into this vast and incomprehensible fleet of worlds with hope? Does our Heavenly Father chide us for so doing, or does He not rather delight in seeing His feeble children climb up the dizzy heights of science and admiringly gaze upon the works of Him whom we are taught to call our Father.

"Our Father who art in Heaven."

Jehovah loves a well-educated mind. With

Him and His children "ignorance is not bliss." 'Tis not "folly to be wise." When by the grand idealization of our mind we add immense distances to our vision by the use of the telescope, bringing not only distant stars nearer to us, but millions of worlds before unknown, He smiles who loves us and He is glorified who gave us being.

Let us then take courage and hasten from the known to the unknown, that we may view the fields where the mighty angels reside and where God is glorified as much in the management of worlds as He is in their formation—as much in angels' work as in that of His anointed Israel.

Before we proceed further, let us take a hasty survey of the solar system. To do so, we will take an Express Train of thought, and travel millions of miles a second and see as much of the wonders of the skies as possible. We must not let our train collide with regular trains; so we will make our first station the sun—95,000,000 of miles away. (The *mean* distance of the sun from the earth is not 95,000,000 of miles, but for convenience we have adopted that reckoning.) Now, all aboard on a straight track to the limits of the solar system. Millions of miles a second we go, but—halt! Here is the regular train on the orbit track of Mercury—

37,000,000 miles. It is as red as fire and its speed is terrible. It passes at 112,000 miles an hour. Its diameter 3,200 miles; day, twenty-four hours, five minutes; year, eighty-eight days.

We are now on a straight line, 37,000,000 miles from the sun. Mercury has passed. All aboard. The next station is Venus, 31,000,000 further on. Look! Yonder comes Venus at 75,000 miles per hour. The diameter of Venus is 7,700 miles; day, twenty-three hours; year, 224 days. We are now 68,000,000 miles from the sun. On again. There, see! Our planet, the earth, is coming at the awful speed of 68,000 miles per hour. Diameter, 7,926 miles. We are now on our straight line, 27,000,000 of miles farther. We are now about 95,000,000 of miles from the sun. On again for a long distance. Stop! We are now on the track of Mars, 142,000,000 of miles from the sun. She rolls by at 55,000 miles per hour. Her diameter is 4,189 miles; day, $23\frac{1}{2}$ hours; year, 321 days.

Still on a much longer trip, 343,000,000 of miles to Jupiter. See! There she comes! Stand aside! She is 1,280 times as large as the earth, and is rolling by at 30,000 miles per hour. She revolves in ten hours; year, nearly twelve of our years. See her great belts of light and dark.

All aboard! We are now 480,000,000 miles from the sun. Our next stopping station will be at the orbit track of Saturn, 800,000,000 miles from our grand luminary. Yonder she comes, 1,100 times larger than the earth, and at the marvelous speed of 22,000 miles per hour. Diameter, 79,000 miles; rotation, 10½ hours; a year is thirty of ours. See, there are two great solid rings around Saturn. The inside ring is 17,000 miles wide, and 19,000 miles off from the body of the planet. The second ring is 18,000 miles farther out, and 10,000 miles in width.

On we go again—ten hundred million miles. We are now 1,800 million miles from the sun, and here comes the planet Herschel or Uranus.

We are now an almost incomprehensible distance from the sun, but still in the Solar System. Uranus is eighty times larger than the earth, and rolls by us at 15,000 miles per hour. She has six moons seen by Herschel, three by other astronomers —these moons moving the opposite way from the Satellites of other Planets.

Our next stopping station is at the boundary of the Solar System. The remotest planet from the sun is Leverier or Neptune, 2,850 millions of miles away. Clear the track! Here comes our last great planet in the Solar System like a "cannon ball" on its heaven laid track—its orbit, and the grandeur of this far off world is indeed indescribable. Here is supposed to be a group of asteroids, and these are the outer limits of the Solar System.

Let us now direct our train of thought for a farther survey of God's wonderful works in the skies. If we look at the heavens from an earth standpoint they appear as a vast concave with innumerable fire specks everywhere; no constellations; no chain; no dependence of one upon another; but it is really not so.

Link intercommunicates with link, constellations with constellations, systems with systems, till we behold, indeed, a vast assemblage of worlds in complete intercourse, balancing and regulating themselves by forces to us unknown. But we ask, can the heavenly bodies be classified, or does the majesty of their motions forbid such a hypothesis? No, indeed. They are already classified, and have been from remotest Biblical antiquity. Astronomers have also classified them by the Biblical or Mystical Seven. Let us observe this astronomical classification of the systems:

First. The Satellite System, or moons revolv-

ing around worlds as our Luna around our earth—
as the moons of Saturn and of Herschel.

Second. The Solar System, or worlds with their Satellites revolving around suns, as in our Solar System.

Third. Sun's Systems; or many Solar Systems like ours revolving with all their attracted orbs and satellites around some grand central sun.

Fourth. Group Systems, or sun's systems with all their Solar Systems, and their appendages revolving around the grand centre of their attraction, forming the centre of thousands of Solar Systems.

Fifth, Cluster Systems, or a grand celestial centre around which thousands of groups are radiating in grandeur incomprehensible and glorious.

Sixth. Nebulæ Systems, or the whole galaxy's centre, around which all the Cluster Systems with all their Group Systems with all their Sun's Systems, with all their Satellite Systems, radiate.

Seventh. The Universal Centre, or the revolving galaxies that radiate around the throne of the Supreme Eternal.

In this wonderful age, when telescopes of marvelous power sweep the heavens, we may greatly increase our knowledge of the sublimity of the skies by a careful survey of the majesty and magnitudes of the heavenly bodies. While so much celestial display is within the reach of our telescopes (that is our powerful telescopes, aided by the spectroscope—which give to us our knowledge that our galaxy—the milky way across the heavens—is a complete system, made up of lesser systems,) we cannot but recognize a still mightier range in these circling beatitudes even of galaxies unknown to us, but constituting other fields of enchantment and wonder.

To look understandingly at the heavenly bodies from such an exalted centre as we conceive the Universe centre must be, we are necessarily forced to associate ourselves with illimitable spaces—with incomprehensible motions. Thus, while we view the heavens as an incomprehensible vessel-fleet of systems, we must also realize that each division accords to another, as in geometry or geography.

We have Districts, Townships, Counties, States, Continents, Hemispheres, and the Globe, each having a central governing power, submissive to the next, embracing a wider range, superlative only by the laws of reciprocal intercourse, whether of Justices, Chief Magistrates, Kings, or Potentates. So of the heavens from Satellite up to the great centre.

To suppose the universe to have no central life-force, or that it is controlled by no intelligent Creator, is to invite into our discussion anarchy or contending equals, chance or confusion, where now undistracted harmony reigns.

On such a hypothesis nothing is immutable or imperishable; but admitting a recognition of the Eternal, the intelligent and infinitely Wise Creator, we are ushered into the reasonable contemplation of revovling worlds and systems in celestial harmony.

Let us, then, admitting an Eternal First Cause by the three steps of Jacob's Ladder, or by the swifter flight or an apostle who was caught up to the third heavens, or as the Revelator saw the heavens open and a voice saying, "Come up hither," avail ourselves of the celestial invitation, and survey, as far as our limited capacity extends, the wonderful works of God throughout the vast unknown.

CHAPTER II.

In our Solar "trip" we took a "train of thought" from the grand Solar Sun straight out in a tangent line to the limits of the Solar System, passing the orbits of Mercury, Venus, Earth, Mars, Jupiter, Saturn, Herschel and Neptune, 2,850 millions of miles from the Sun; and here we found the ultima thulæ of the Solar System.

Then admitting an Eternal First Cause, and being invited as we supposed by a holy angel to "Come up hither" in our train of thought, we hasted to obey, by preparing ourselves for the wonderful journey to the Skies.

Leaning then on the word of the Great Messiah, "Fear Not," we are now ready to fly beyond the known, to the unknown.

But before we start, let us ask ourselves, "Is there such a place as heaven?" A place where Christ is all and in all; where the saints of all ages are to meet and forever celebrate the glories of King Immanuel, and view that particular locality of which He spoke when He said: "I will prepare a Mansion for you, that where I am there ye may be also." If we are fully convinced that there is such a "City," such a "Home," such a "Place," in a realm beyond the reach of telescopes, a country only explored by faith, then surely we are invited to climb this Jacob's Ladder, and view the promised land.

Enchantment of wonders! the land of "Beulæ!" the "great white throne," the "consuming fire" of glory's eternal brightness.

Here, at the great Centre of all centres, we may gaze upon the Light producing source of all moral and intellectual light—the Light that illuminates all moral sensibility, of all sentient intelligences.

Here also is the Centre of Holiness. The Holy Spirit's great, grand Centre. Here is Life's Centre. God is the author of life. All moral and celestial intelligences owe their being to the Author of Life. He who here resides.

Here also resides the centre of all equity. Justice—the God of Justice. Here we behold, through the door of Mercy, the God of Mercy.

The well-spring of the hopes of the trangressors for whom pardon is offered through the infinitely

Merciful. This throne is indeed Mercy's Centre.

Here are the pavillions of eternal Truth. The God of all Truth resides here. And the crowning glory of this Great Centre is that a God of Love occupies this Throne of Grace.

This is indeed the celestial council chamber of the great God; the central abode of Wisdom, Majesty and Power; the "Dwelling Place" of the great, grand Master.

Faint conceptions of this "Great White Throne" are revealed to us by the prophets—brilliant gems are divinely unfolded to us from the lips of the Great Messiah, but the overwhelming display of the "Light Unapproachable" no thought can reach —no imagination paint. An uprush of incandescent Light surrounds the throne of the great "I Am," and no intelligence can behold with steadfast gaze this awful Majesty and burning splendor.

If Mount Sinai was "terrible" to behold, when Jehovah deigned to bring together a few of the rays of His Omnipotent Self—if Moses could say " I exceedingly fear and quake," how terrible indeed must be His glory, at this great grand Center. From hence emanates all power, and at this centre all wisdom dwells.

We feel forbidden by the very laws of our being, to introduce a single question as to the Entity, Sovereignty or Eternity of God.

As visitors to this "Mount of God," let us behold His immutability at the centre of these limitless spaces that surround the Throne; for if there is a place that is immovable, it must be where Infinite strength resides.

In every conceivable direction from this Centre, myriad Worlds and Systems and Galaxies are visible.

What a vast Panorama is spread out before us; what grandeur, what order, what terrible display.

Our chariot of thought must soon pass on, but stop and look a moment longer. What a vast retinue of semi-Deities (we almost say) receive their "orders" from this great White Throne—no wonder the great minded Revelator could mistake one of these and fall down to "worship Him." They are so God-like, so super-human.

But see! They haste away on orders as incomprehensible to us as is their motions of fleetness, when compared with our slow tread while climbing the rugged mountains of this mundane orb.

But because unknown to us, shall we assert that God has nothing for Angels to do!

Angels are but links in the chain between God and Matter—between Omnipotent life force and mechanical force.

The vitalization of motion must be kept active by life-force, for no other force is exhaustless, and as God has formed all matter—all Worlds, the vital force to operate this vast Machine, must have been committed to active, sentient Intelligences.

Now, being at the place designated as the Christian's Home, let us look for a moment at the "Many Mansions" in the city of the "New Jerusalem" which the Revelator saw as coming down from Heaven all decked in superlative glory "as a bride adorned for her husband."

As we have read before starting on our "Trip to the Skies" a full description of the foundations, the gates—the gems of Glory that adorn its finish—the golden streets—the silver fountain—the River of Life and its purifying power—we have only to visit the "Many Mansions," and then pursue our journey amidst the wonderful galaxies of the skies.

The first wonderful Mansion is that of Light—No sun opens the morn or closes the evening with its silvery sitting, but one great, grand Mansion of

Light. Light to the hitherto darkened soul. Light in God's Light.

O how the shadows of our dreamy life are chased away as we enter this Mansion. We rejoice in the faith of our pilgrimage which said "It may not be my way, it may not be thy way, but in His own dear way, the Lord will provide." But as we cannot enter this Mansion of Light, so we cannot learn all that we now wish to know, but will wait for the Angels to come with their chariot, in the near future, with a free Passport into that Mansion of Light, and then we shall forever exult in its glory.

See! Yonder is the Mansion of Life. O how we shall rejoice to know that our names are written in the "Book of Life." Here the life of God actuates every guest, and His knowledge qualifies us for this "life to come"—this life which we now live in the flesh which is "hid with Christ in God."

"That life which Thou hast made Thy care,
Lord I devote to Thee."

But look again! There is the Mansion of Holiness. O how glorious—Holy beings without a stain enter, and reside in this Mansion, and were it not for the fountain you see yonder flowing from the "Throne of God and the Lamb," we could never enter this Holy place. So we are only permitted to see "as in a glass" this Holy! Holy!! Holy!!! Mansion.

Let us now visit the Mansion of Justice. How exceedingly high are its walls, how equitable all its decisions. We ask how can we enter this glorious Mansion? The answer comes from our Celestial R. R. Guide Book "The Just shall Live by Faith." If Christ is formed in us, the hope of glory where he enters we may enter, but now our Passport is not sealed, so we will wait. O how beautiful is the Mansion of Mercy. Here are acclamations of thanksgiving—of praise and of glory, to a God of Mercy.

But yonder is the Mansion of Truth, in which is found the Eternal Oracles of God—the celestial decisions from which there is no appeal.

Look a moment at the Mansion of Love, where centers Eternal constancy, and then we will leave this glorious City, and view the wonders of the Skies.

CHAPTER III.

Nebulæ System.

We will now leave this citadel of God having seen the "Many Mansions" in the New Jerusalem, shortly to descend from God out of Heaven "as a bride adorned for her husband," but could not enter these Celestial Mansions, being only invited to "come up hither," not to enter that Eternal rest.

Let us now look afar and behold this vast mechanism of the Skies, to us inexpressibly wonderful; and intuitively we ask, will "the Seven Spirits of God" ever unseal this Book of Wonders? Must it forever be as it now appears—these stellar orbs changing and reforming, like jets of gas in a great City, as we sweep on our night train around its grand display; some apparently receeding and some advancing; some in long rows as sentinels, and anon all joined in one general blaze of light. So now of the Heavens, when thus on one of these moving orbs, we sweep around the great, grand center of Celestial Magnitudes. All is in motion —but how?

But now, on our grand excursion train of thought, as we have stopped at the terminus of immutability, let us look abroad. Can we comparatively master the field? Can we realize that the great Nebulæ System, composed, as we have seen, of Cluster Systems, Group Systems, Sun's Systems, Solar Systems and Satellite Systems, is itself but a Single System, and in comparison with other Systems, composed of Systems in like manner with itself, may indeed be inferior to them, as our Earth is inferior to the Sun around which it revolves? How exceedingly vast the distances—how innumerable the hosts of worlds—of Systems—of Celestial Nebulæ.

All revolving Worlds have fixed boundaries and well regulated orbits, as well as laws governing their daily and yearly motions.

But who vitalizes this stupendous whole; this unvarying rotation?

Some might say Chance, others, Attraction and Projection; some, Force. But who created Chance, Attraction, Projection, Force?

Where have we found machinery in motion, without intelligent agencies to regulate and direct it? And is not the stellar skies one vast machine? Could we think, that some day the Sun would forget to shine, the Moon forget to ride across the heavens in its full blaze of glory? Dark, dark unending night cover our Planet? This is indeed unthinkable, so long as the great Celestial Ruler harmonizes and vitalizes the whole. If corn would not plant itself by attraction, chance or force; if railroads could not lay their own track and originate their engines without intelligent workmen, how could our Earth lay its track, its orbit, and take with it the ponderous Moon on its annual and diurnal motion? Surely reason does not accord to such an insane idea. Mechanism supposes the mechanic, as well as the operatives, to control the machinery.

God rules over the children of men, as he does over the work of angels, and has an abundance of business for angels to do, as he also bids us, "Go work in my vineyard." So Angels have work to do, and these great and grand motions of the heavenly bodies witness to that department of angelic labor—" the mighty angel's" work.

God works, angels work, and man is commanded to work. Jesus says: "My Father hitherto worked, and I work'" God's great domain requires the work of both mortal and spiritual intelligences.

So the field where Angels labor, is, and must be, a vast field. God needs them or he would not have created them, and, although they are dual beings, while we are triune, yet in their field, they are as neccesary, as are we to the earth we are commanded to replenish.

In one sense, God governs absolutely the destiny of nations. A nation could be destroyed in a single day as easily as an individual, but in His supreme wisdom He holds his dynamic forces from such an awful calamity, and nations increase and prosper. In one sense, He also holds the destiny of Angels, yet each have their work over which no unseen fatality predominates.

If Angels govern the activities of these myriad worlds, there must of necessity be an "innumerable company of the Angels," for, in the management of this one Nebulæ System at which we are now directing our attention, aided by the telescope in our Celestial survey, an exceedingly great host is necessary. The arranging of orbits—the equation of power in attraction and repulsion—the rapidity of motion, all need attention, wisdom, order. And should the solar gasses evolve and diminish from exhaustion, an eliptic comet must safely cross the track of worlds and supply the needed power. So many Systems, such vast and ponderous orbs to fly through the realms of space, such inconceivable activities in variety—marvelous, yet harmonious—demand the labors of the mighty angels.

How wonderful now to see, not only the motion and regularity of these flying orbs, but the Engineers and Managers of this vast machine. Only one single Nebulæ System demands a host of the Celestial Cherubim, Seraphim, Angels and Archangels, so that everywhere in the midst of these startling activities, we behold harmony, concord, connection—an endless chain of harmonies.

But yonder, look! Other Nebulæ Systems, equally vast, are circling around their centers in as perfect harmony as does our Earth around the Sun, and now to us, as we look out from this exalted station, we can distinguish the boundaries of these vast magnitudes from other Nebulæ, as we do Jupiter with his four Moons, Saturn with his eight, or the Earth with her Luna.

From hence, we look upon these revolving clusters of galaxies, as we now look upon a single

Solar System or group. How vast the contemplation. Millions upon millions of galaxies appear at every point from this wonderful center. No marvel, that the Revelator spoke of the host that peopled these realms, as "thousands of thousands, and ten thousand times ten thousand"—a host "that no man could number."

What a field for the armies of the Heavens, when we realize that the motions of these vast Systems in their circling harmonies around these great, grand centers, must have been committed to these mighty messengers of the Most High. Who else?

We see a steamer far out on the lake, plodding its way onward, and though so far from us that we do not discover a person on board, still we say, who other than man, manages this steamer.

How strange when gazing at the terrific fleetness of a passing world, we should doubt the managing necessity, of sentient intelligencies. How could the "heavens declare the Glory of God" only through the celestial messengers that manage these rotations under the Divine Superintendence.

Illimitable galaxies startle us, and we gaze with wonder and inexplicable awe, as we behold the field of these mighty angels, who, with the fleetness of thought direct the revolving machinery of the great God, in accordance with His Divine command.

Here now, let us look again and ask, is this the "City of the Great King," the "City of God," the "New Jerusalem," the "Home of the Church of the First Born, the Bride of Christ?"

> "Oh, glorious day! Oh, blessed hope!
> My heart leaps forward at the thought,
> When in that happy, happy land,
> We'll no more take the parting hand."

Ah, reader, will you and I re-visit this Glorious Home in an angel chariot, instead of this excursion train of Faith? Will we indeed enter these Mansions and dwell in this "Palace of God" forever? Will the few more years of life fit us for that Eternal Home, having our sins washed away through the "Fountain filled with Blood," and our "Robes made White in the Blood of the Lamb?"

We shall see, bye and bye.

Our next trip will take us into the grand Nebulæ System to explore the fields that astronomers faintly see through our powerful telescopes.

CHAPTER IV.

Our Nebulæ System.

Reader, can you by any possible reflection consider the very slender thread that binds us to these Solar skies; and can you for a moment measure an Eternity of duration elsewhere, and contrast the greatness of that duration with the uncertainty of this? If you possibly can do so, you will at best only grasp an Eternity of fancy—not the great reality of unchanging duration.

To be happy with the great—the learned—the mighty, we must ourselves be competent to that association. Children, though destitute of manhood strength, may join in the general joy, when some mighty achievement has been accomplished by a stronger brother, and we do not hesitate to accord to them the right to rejoice, because it is in the nature of legitimate kindred to do so.

Are we the legitimate kindred of those to whom, in the hour of dissolving ties, we look for, as our guardian angels, to ferry us over the dark, cold stream of death? On what do we base a conclusion of such vast magnitude? How fearful to be in great peril, where no one can help us—a ship at sea, on fire, and we helpless, on board.

Now, we in our train of thought, have supposed ourselves safe in traveling up the Christian's highway of song and celestial gladness, have dismissed our fears; have ignored our peril; have, like our polar exploration parties, looked forward to a glorious return, and have not dared to reflect upon the awful fields of limitless duration, where our compass gives no tangible direction, our vision falls on no familiar star, our little all, on the billowy archipelago of the unknown, and we flying through the unknown in our fancy-formed chariot of thought.

Look away across the orbits of galaxies, and then add telescope to telescope, till all of earth, have added distances to incomprehensible distances, and is there not a star, a group, a system of worlds beyond? Surely the end is unthinkable, either of space or planets.

Then whither will we fly, and who will lead us out into fields so fearfully vast, that, should we attempt the journey alone, we may be eternally lost in the bewilderment of unsurveyed galaxies? Have we a friend here who could send a servant to accompany us outside of "the highway cast up for the ransomed of the Lord to walk in"—the way we came to this city; that we might safely start again on our sidereal trip through the skies? Yes. The poet has sung it thus—"What a friend we have in Jesus."

And this friend is here "preparing mansions for them that love him," and if we ask, He will send His angel to accompany us on our celestial exploration.

Having obtained a heavenly escort, let us haste on in thought's rapid express train at trillions of miles a second, into the ultimathule of the Creator's works.

Angel guide, please take us to that brilliant fixed star in the constellation of Bootes. Ah, we are at Arcturus, away in the heavens, not less than nineteen trillion of miles from the earth we inhabit. How inconceivable the distance, (19,000,000,000,000.) Now, suppose the whole orbit of the earth were a dark, opaque body, 183,000,000 miles across, it would become only a speck not half as large as the letter "o" in the type used in this sketch, when seen from the fixed star, Arcturus.

We are apt to be led astray by the term "fixed

star," and suppose these stars are stationary in the skies, but they are all in motion, and the farther off they are, it seems only to increase the rapidity of their motion through the heavens.

Arcturus, one of the fixed stars, is rolling through space at the terrible rate of two hundred thousand miles (200,000) per hour.

A few chapters back, we were almost terrified to see the little planet, Mercury, roll past us at one hundred and twelve thousand miles (112,000) per hour, but here is a fixed star of a diameter almost incomprehensible, hurrying on at nearly twice the speed of our second door neighbor, between us and the Sun, Mercury.

Now these fixed stars must be great suns, around which radiate a vast retinue of worlds, and where is the track—the orbit of Arcturus? If, advancing in the earth's orbit, in our sweep around the Sun, we approach one hundred and eighty-three millions of miles nearer a fixed star, a parrallax, as Prof. Airy asserts, shows an increase of the star equal to only six-tenths of an inch a mile distant, how inconceivably vast must be the distance then, between the astronomer and the star he is trying to develope. Then again, while this star is moving through space at the rate of 200,000 miles an hour, it would be three hundred years in changing its position 2,000 miles on its vast orbit.

We mentioned Arcturus in the Northern Constellation of the Bootes, as our stopping place. Our readers are aware that the Greek letters are used to denote the stars of the various apparent magnitudes—hence Alpha, Beta, Gamma, Delta, etc. These letters do not give the idea of the magnitudes of the sidereal worlds, for that is impossible, for our greatest telescopes fail to discover a disk or any tangible clew to their magnitudes—their brightness only, is thus designated. Stars of the first, second and third magnitudes in the Greek alphabetical letters, instead of 1, 2, 3, etc.

There must be startling wonders in these heavens, and our readers will be curious to know of what advantage it can be to us to take this "Trip to the Skies" when we cannot comprehend the distances, magnitudes and motions of these vast and ponderous orbs. Why, my dear reader, these are our reasons:

First, we have a father in heaven.

"Our Father who art in Heaven."

These orbs were made by him:

"He made the Stars also."—Gen., i. xvi.

We are his offspring and in his legacy we inherit

a relation to his works. This world is not our eternal home, for we tarry only our three score years and ten and then we pass away.

Second. Somewhere in these Heavens, the saints of all ages will meet in the brightness of the glory of the only begotten Son of God.

Third. We are commanded to "search out the deep things of God." We owe to God this tribute of our intellect.

Hence, in thought, let us pass beyond the telescope's range, and from the books of Revelation and Philosophy, explore the hidden mysteries of the vastness of unexplored galaxies.

It is quite probable that in the days of Job, astronomy was far in advance of the present. In the questions asked Job in reference to the Pleiades, Mazzaroth, Arcturus, and Orion, the supposition is that he understood the majesty, motion, and influences of the stars and constellations. (See Job, xxxviii: 31-2.) If so, we have failed as much in our telescopic achievements, as did the inventor of the lumber wagon and common highway, fail as to speed with the railroad passenger coach, drawn by a powerful engine.

"Canst thou bring forth Mazzaroth in his season, or canst thou guide Acturus with his sons."— Job xxxviii: 31.

Job refers quite familiarly to these mighty stars in the following language:

"He shaketh the earth out of her place and the pillars thereof tremble. He commandeth the sun and it riseth not, and sealeth up the stars. He alone spreadeth out the heavens and treadeth upon the waves of the sea. He maketh Arcturus, Orion and Pleiades, and the Chambers of the South. He doeth great things past finding out; yea, and wonders without number."

This wonderfully brilliant star, Arcturus, is in the constellation of the bear-driver, Bootes, who, like a mountain-range hunter, holds in the grasp of his right hand a huge club, and by his left, guides his fierce hounds in a continuous chase of the great bear as he hastes around the polar star. You will discover this magnificent star in the left knee of this monster man Bootes. It formes two triangles with other fixed stars, namely: Denebola and Spica, and also Denebola and Cor-Caroli.

The "Sons of Arcturus" as adverted to in the Almighty's question to Job, are probably Spica, Denebola, Cor-Caroli, and Segimus, these all being arranged in right angles and triangles with Arcturus. The mythology that accompanies these constellations, is so mixed up with procreation that no tangible fact accompanies their history. It would appear from this reading of Greek and Roman Mythology that constellations were intelligent persons, male and female, and marriages and births were common among the stars. Indeed, a very strange phenomenon. We only advert to these imaginary constellations the better to locate the Grand Centres of the sidereal universe, and as to the sex; be it bear, or wolf, or dog, or under any other name whereby sex or procreation are supposed to occur, we dissent. The great astronomer, Laplace, advanced a theory about the origin of the Solar System, which, if true, might apply to other systems and give us the idea that great planets surrounded by vast nebulæs of gas may throw off rings which might condense into worlds, and so continue to advance in multiplying numbers till the whole nebulæ become opaque bodies, local in orbits, formed by attraction and projection, or by attractive and repellant forces.

These worlds or orbs being produced from the gaseous surrroundings of Arcturus may properly have been called the "Sons of Arcturus," conveying the idea that the great planet once encircled them all in his own sidereal orbit. This could have no reference to sex or gender, to wars or marriages.

Our readers are aware that our point of observation is from a fixed star of Biblical antiquity, and that this star is in one of the Northern Circumpolar Constellations. This Constellation is always visible to our gaze, of a clear night, at any season of the year, and it is hoped by the writer that our readers will cast an eye northward, and if possible, discover the Great Bear, as well as Arcturus, so that in our further trip across the heavens we may become at least familiar with the Sailor's Dipper, whose "pointers" you may discover in the body of the Great Bear, while his long tail furnishes a convenient handle by which you may recognize and determine the Pole Star from all other fixed stars in the heavens.

CHAPTER V.

OUR NEBULÆ SYSTEM.

"It is sown in weakness; It is raised in power."--*Paul.*

"There's a Divinity that shapes our ends,
Rough hew them how we will."

O Life! a span at longest thread,
Speed swiftly on with stately tread,
   To regions vast, unknown;
We try to scan the darkened vale,
And not discouraged, though we fail,
   Our faith, in weakness sown.

But when the Pearly gates we see,
Beyond the earth-born destiny,
   On Heaven's unending shore;
Our bodies free from weakness given,
Then bright the vale—the joys of Heaven,
   Ah! blessed forevermore.

There's brighter worlds—far, far away,
Where darkness never clouds the day,
   Nor sorrows reach the shore;
Where blessed in Loves celestial chain,
Where parted loved ones meet again,
   And shout life's weakness o'er.

At Arcturus, in the Constellation of Bootes—away, away; so far that thought in his lightning chariot, tires in the endless survey. Now, suppose that we actually had a railroad track from Arcturus' home, and the fare was one cent for each hundred miles, how much money would it require to puschase a ticket? Astonishing! One cent for each hundred miles would cost five billion, six hundred and seventy-eight million dollars. Pretty costly trip that! At the end of the war "Uncle Sam" found his debt to be three billion, eight hundred million dollars. That would only pay our fare a little over half-way home at the rate of one-tenth of a mill per mile. Surely Arcturus is very far off.

If Arcturus should suddenly disappear, we should see it as it now appears for twenty-six years to come, for it took all that long period for light to travel to us from this vastly distant star.

Thought is the swiftest messenger known, and it is indeed wonderful how swiftly it passes from star to star, from constellation to constellation and from galaxy to galaxy, until the whole heavens have passed in review before us, yet we have only THOUGHT.

The power, that gave us this power, must be equal to the highest conception of fleetness that our minds possess; hence no power less than the Infinite could have fashioned man. We then possess the infinite, for thought is as infinite, as space or duration, and hence an agent infinite, like his Creator, must be infinitely responsible to his Creator during his eternity of being.

Another misapprehension is liable to spring up in our minds in reference to all the stars going around the Pole Star. To us it so appears, and to us all, the Nebulæ System appears to be going around our little earth, but it is not so. The motion of the earth as it passes through the skies, changes the appearance of all the stars. Even the North Star becomes higher up or lower down in the heavens at different periods. And so of the fixed stars.

We once heard a clergyman illustrating before his audience, the wonders of the skies in this manner:

"You see, brethren and sisters, the unchangeable purposes of God, in the motion of the Great Bear and the Sailors' Dipper as they pass around the Polar Star from night to night continually.

"Now, my brethren, the stars in the Great Bear's long tail, are a great deal farther off from the North Star, than are the pointers, and you see must go faster to keep up; and yet my brethren, the handle of the dipper remains just as crooked as it is, from year to year, and oh! my brethren, should Gabriel stand with one foot on the sea and the other on the land, and grasp the Great Bear by his long tail, and slash worlds against worlds, what would we poor sinners do? Won't the brethren and sisters sing a hymn?"

We are easily deceived, in looking up into the skies, if we expect to observe stars and constellations as they really are, for the reason that we too, are borne along at a terrible rapid rate.

Is it possible for us to explore this mighty orb —Arcturus?

Only in reason and fancy can we go farther than astronomical apparatus will extend our vision, but it must be admitted that we have found the star designated in the Almighty's question to Job. So we know this star has extraordinary wonders, either in its inhabitants, or its motions, or its greatness. Maybe all these make it a notable star. If we take the Royal Astronomer's parallax— Prof. Airy, as a guide—we shall find it at least one million miles in diameter, and yet we lack the power to grasp a disk, or visible face, or projection from which to make a correct astronomical observation. It must, in the nature of things, be greatly farther away than nineteen trillions of miles.

But no matter as to the exact distance. We look above, and around, and the same arch of heaven surrounds us, and the stars shine in their twinkling brilliancy. The Milky way is no nearer; the constellations just as diffused throughout the heavenly arch; the fixed stars shining no less brightly than from the earth we inhabit.

But what shall we say of the inhabitants of Arcturus? They may be in form like ourselves. There are many reasons why we should thus believe. First, all the children of God must possess all the attributes of God, and as the man, Christ Jesus possessed the human form, to be like him' they must possess a similar form; and as all angels ever seen are of that form, it is supposable that the inhabitants of Arcturus possess the same.

And what can we recognize at Arcturus the same as here. We may recognize the seven Attributes of God here as elsewhere. "God is Light;" light is here. God is Holiness; holiness is here. God is Justice; justice is here. God is Mercy; mercy is here. God is Truth; truth is here. God is Love; love is here.

D

Then if beings in form like ourselves, possessing attributes like ourselves, are here, we certainly can be happy in their company, provided the seven tones of music are in this element as it is in the atmosphere of earth. Certainly angels sing, and why should there be a world without singing. By these vibrations, all languages, dialects and idioms find utterance. O! the song of redemption is music everywhere. Then the seven prismatic colors are seen in the stars as through our telescopes from an earthly observatory. Yellow, green, orange, violet, indigo, red and blue, which, with the beautiful rainbow minglings, are seen in the Southern Cross, and widely scattered throughout the vast expanse. This adds beauty to the arch of heaven and variety to the colors of celestial scenery, and above all, it is God's universal monogram—"I made it."

We then conclude that if Arcturus is inhabited, that its citizens must have heard of Jesus of Nazareth, and are in essential love with him and all his children.

"Let all the angels of God worship Him."

Ah! To stay here with the sinless and happy, and to rehearse the glad tidings of salvation in these celestial choirs, away from pain, old age, sorrow, sin, suffering and death; who would not count such a resort the great centre of the soul's highest delight?

Now suppose that we have had three distinct dispensations of time, and that these periods are of equal duration, and when full will amount to 12,000 years. "The woman had on her head a a crown of twelve stars." The first dispensation to be that of Purity—the sinless of our first parents peopled and replenished the earth for four thousand years, till a host that "no man could number," were transported to the skies, and Eden planted and Adam and the woman placed in the garden of temptation, where they dared to taste of that forbidden tree in the midst of the garden of God.

While still surrounded by some of the sinless of their vast progeny not transported for some cause, they (our first parents) sinned, and thereby brought death into the world. Then commenced the second dispensation—that of Types. This continued until the offering up of Christ on the Cross—4,000 years.

Then the dispensation of Grace commenced and will continue 4,000 years.

Of this transported church—"the church of the first born, whose names are written in heaven"—

we know but little. Their monuments remain a wonder to the geologists everywhere—but no name, history or record anywhere. It might be possible that in this far off star, we shall find part at least of this host.

These are the sinless ones of earth, whose long residence on our planet will make them to us a joy and rejoicing, while our victory over death—the king of tyrants—through the blood of the Lamb, will increase their joy in our company. Delightful thought! We have an eternity to spend in the skies, and the greatness of the preparation for such an event, should inspire us with intense zeal to labor and secure a prize so vast, so precious. We ask our readers the question—around what centre does Arcturus radiate?

CHAPTER VI.

Circumpolar Constellations.

It is generally supposed that the circumpolar constellations radiate around the pole star as their great celestial centre. Many thousand readers, who well know the "pointers" in the Sailor's Dipper have never learned their names, and perhaps are not aware that they have any distinct names. They are named Dubhe and Merak. They are always visible in northern latitudes from the fact that the earth hangs in the heavens at 23½ degrees from a perpendicular to its orbit, and in perfect range with the Polaris or pole star, hence the axis of the earth sustains itself in a parallel to itself, and rarely varies from having the north and south pole constantly in range of line with the pole star or Polaris. Were it not for this obliquity of the eliptic, we could have no variety of seasons.

If Arcturus is in the constellation of Bootes, (one of the circumpolar constellations) it must of necessity radiate around the great Polaris. If this be so, its orbit must be of almost infinite circumference, and being understood by God's ancient servant, Job, in the majesty of its magnitude and motions, no doubt this greatly humiliated him in the presence of its Creator. "Cans't thou guide Arcturus and his sons?"—Job 38-32. What a question to propound to a poor frail mortal.

If on examination as to the size of Arcturus our telescopes could afford us no disk, and consequently no accurate clew to its diameter, how sadly deficient we are when we attempt to traverse its orbit as it passes on its long journey around the yellow North Star. If at 200,000 miles an hour it would take three hundred years to change its position 2,000 miles as seen in its circle from our earth, what an almost infinite sweep it must take, and who but Him that formed it, could fully understand its fearful surroundings. We had supposed that it might be inhabited by a sinless race, (for Astronomy furnishes no evidence that the "war in Heaven" extended farther than our Solar System,) and if so, then we might multiply the inhabitants of the sidereal skies into an infinity so to speak, and then transgress no logical deduction that might be drawn from revelation or from reason. Surely in thought, we are not forbidden to explore the realms of Arcturus and his sons, and

He that bade us take in this gigantic orb, will be the last to fault us, in the absence of other methods of conveyance, if we travel in a train of thought.

Analogical logic, may furnish some basis of argument as to the people that might be now engaged in this celestial labor, in drawing our conclusions. If God anxiously urged our first parents to multiply and replenish the earth, then the bringing into existence of holy beings must be pleasing to his sight. Other worlds demand for the declarative glory of God, an unnumbered host of sentient intelligences, therefore other worlds must be populated. The analogy in this logical deduction is neither far fetched nor chimerical, and must, when addressed to the thinking, appear with some degree of truthfulness. God's great commands, purposes and promises, not to speak of his revelation as to the multitudes in Heaven, all incline to this analogical reasoning, viz: that the stars are peopled with millions of millions.

If so, "Arcturus and his sons" may be the abode of an unnumbered host of celestial intelligences. Then again the name of Arcturus for the star, may have originated from the superior excellence of some mighty angel whose achievements honored God, and he named this star after this mighty intelligence, as Columbia was named after Columbus—the great discoverer; or the star Leverier, after the distinguished doctor and Astronoomer who first discovered it.

Undoubtedly the Almighty had reference to the star, and not to an individual creature, when he addressed Job.

There are many promises to the faithful to show the design of God to transfer much of the power, now entrusted to Angels, to his redeemed people at the close of the present dispensation—the dispensation of Grace.

"Thou hast been faithful over a few things; I will make thee ruler over many things; enter thou into the joy of thy Lord." Matt. 25-23.

If a ruler, it must imply to rule sentient intelligences, or the management of worlds, or both. Such a glory as this is worth living for, especially when the path of holiness is the path of peace.

Now if Arcturus is nineteen trillions of miles from the earth, how far must he be from the North Star? If we could, to a positive certainty, ascertain the diameter of the orbit of Arcturus, we might possibly find the distance to its centre, by which we might answer the question.

Let me propose a mathematical problem to those of our readers who are versed in figures, and let them take time to answer the question—what is the approximate diameter of the orbit of Arcturus? First, this star is moving through space (so astronomers tell us) at the terrible speed of 200,000 miles an hour. On a tangent line this orbit circle varies the position of Arcturus in 300 years, to the extent of 2,000 miles. What then must be the circumference or diameter of its orbit? Who can tell? These are the only land marks yet discovered.

From analogy we may draw another conclusion—the Earth is larger than the Moon, that revolves around it; the Sun is larger than all of the planets that revolve around it, and, analogically, the the North Star must be larger than all the Circumpolar orbs. There is a wonderful potency or power thrown off from Polaris. Our Earth, at an almost inconceivable distance from this star, is balanced and held in position by it, during all its long journey of 183,000,000 miles while passing around the Sun. At no time does he lose his power over our Earth, notwithstanding the Sun holds an almost absolute potency over its light, heat and motion. It is held by astronomers that our brilliant noonday Sun, is himself with his entire retinue of planets, satellites and asteroids, hurrying on his orbit around the North Star, in association with other constellations, as our Earth is hurrying around the Sun, in association with Jupiter and Saturn.

It is indeed strange that the stars in the stellar skies should partake of all the seven prismatic colors, as they appear to us while looking at them through the telescope. Red, Blue, Yellow, Orange, Violet, Indigo and Green. In some constellations, all of these colors appear.

The "sons of Arcturus" may be moons for aught we know, and not those stars holding the relations of angles and triangles to itself, and if so, our Astronomical appliances afford us no clew by which to solve the problem.

Before we visit Polaris, let us journey to Orion, and if possible, discover "the bands of Orion."

"Cans't thou loose the bands of Orion?" Job, 38-31.

It will be remembered that the outlines of the celestial constellation, Orion, are revealed in a parallelogram of four very brilliant stars. The reader will look for Orion amongst the Equatorial Constellations.

CHAPTER VII.

ORION.

We were about leaving Arcturus in the circumpolar constellation of Bootes, for Orion, one of the equatorial constellations, to ascertain, if possible, what were the "Bands of Orion."

Speaking of constellations, some of our readers may not know how to understand that word. In this manner, perhaps you can better understand it. There are all over the heavens on a clear night, many clusters of stars, some larger than others, but always seen grouped or clustered together. To refer to these understandingly, we must give them a name, and instead of giving them names as we do in geography, as mountains, hills, valleys, oceans, lakes, rivers, continents, hemispheres and globes, we call them constellations, and name them from animals and characters, as the Great Bear, Bootes, etc. There are now in the Heavens ninety-nine constellations, viz: The Zodiacal Constellations, twelve in number; the Northern or Circumpolar Constellations, forty-one in number, and the

Southern Constellations, forty-six in number. A very great proportion of these receive their names from the animal world, as the Swan, Lesser Bear, Serpent, Lion, etc.

The science of constellations is called astrognosy, and dawned upon the world at such an age, that we hardly know who first named them, or why they bear any name at all, especially when we can by no stretch of imagination discover the least possible resemblance between the stars and the animals from which astronomers were pleased to name them. Egyptians, Greeks, Romans, Chinese and Japanese vied with each other to attain the highest perfection of a knowledge of the stars, and to obtain some new conception of their relation to the life and happiness of mortals, and at one time, astrology was considered a safer counsellor to consult in many of the important problems of life, than ever has been modern spiritualism. But we have an earlier birth-place of astronomy than Egypt or Greece, if we consult the book of Job.

Again and again astronomers have tried to change the names of the constellations, but without success. It seems so interwoven with mythology, both in Greek and Roman glory, both in prose and song, that in modern times we leave the myths, as a very senseless way of giving the origin of the names of the heavenly constellations, and had much rather allude to the Sailor's Dipper, the stars giving some outline of such a dish. Surely we can see nothing resembling the Great Bear.

Osiris and Isis—the Sun and the Moon—were noted deities amongst the Egyptians, and they also classified the heavens into mansions, where their numerous Gods resided, and were really a nation of polytheists, or the worshipers of many Gods. Modern astronomers choose to retain nearly all of the mythical constellations, adding thereto such new constellations as by our access to greater telescopes appear in the unlimited spaces of the Heavens. As we journey from Arcturus in our fleet chariot of thought, ten thousand wonders will startle us into awe and admiration. We can save ourselves much fear by remembering that our Father made these stars and constellations, and that He loves us, and will govern them in accordance with His unchanging love for His children.

From our chariot window, let us look abroad as we journey along the equatorial line south-eastward to Orion. Yonder to the left is the constellation of Ursa Major—the Great Bear. It contains one hundred and thirty-eight stars that are visible to the human eye from Earth, but now in the Heavens how wonderfully grand they appear. This constellation has been celebrated from time immemorial, by not only the Chaldean Shepherds of thousands of years past, who in feasts and dances made Earth vocal by songs and triumphant celebrations, but also, by the American Iroquois Indians, who have not only celebrated it with grand festivities, but have given it the same name as the Chaldeans of bible days, the Great Bear—Ursa Major. But now look as we are passing. There is one star in this constellation that has a planetary nebulæ—a fringe, so to speak, of minute stars—that must embrace a space much larger than the entire orbit of Neptune, or an "island universe" of two or three trillions of miles in diameter. What a terrible array of worlds and systems! How infinite are the creations of the Great God. All through the spaces explored by the mighty sweep of the telescope, we see these innumerable fleets of stars, as a universe dependent upon some central star. Twenty-six of these are already discovered, but only one in Ursa Major. Multiplied by our near approach by millions of magnitudes, how exceedingly grand this "island universe" must appear. The constellation off to our right is Virgo, with angel wings and dressed in celestial splendor. Upon her head may be seen the wonder of wonders so often seen elsewhere, viz: that of two or three great suns revolving in close proximity around each other. Just before us and a little to the left, is Leo—the Lion. He has his cub, the lesser Leo, close by his side, and is adorned with a majesty of stars. In his breast and neck a belt of the most magnificent stars give the perfect outline of a sickle, and his baby lion has two grand clusters, one near his heart and lungs and the other clenched by both his paws, by which his attitude indicates an immediate attack upon the terrible Hydra, who precedes him a little, and carries in his hissing mouth and exalted head a brilliant constellation of flaming Suns. We cannot stop to number these Suns for it would take a lifetime to do so, and then the magnitudes are so vast, that we now, in this life, can obtain no conception of their wonderful majesty. Off to our left as we are now traveling the equatorial line, we can see the constellation of Cancer, and also that of the Cohis Minor—the lesser Dog. This latter is a beautiful constellation of magnificent stars, above which we discover Gemini, or the two beautiful twin babies, whose heads are adorned with the glory of the stars. Hershel describes it, "like gazing into a casket of gems."

Our last constellation as we pass on is the Unicorn. After looking a moment at the beautiful colored stars so apparent in this nebulæ, we arrive at our journey's end, the constellation of the grand and majestic Orion. We have now crossed the Heavens from Arcturus to Orion, millions of trillions of miles in our rapid express train of thought, and have only looked to wonder, to be more than amazed at the "glory of the stars," keeping all the time regulated by the facts revealed to us through the telescope.

"Cans't Thou loose the bands of Orion." Job, 38-31.

We mentioned that many of the stars were double Suns, revolving around each other as our Moon revolves around the Earth. Only here we have suns of unknown magnitude revolving around each other, as in Lyra, we, with the naked eye, see only one star, but with the telescope we see two great suns, in close proximity to each other, passing around each other in awful grandeur. As before remarked, we can discover no disk, so we cannot tell the exact size of these brilliant orbs. You see in the dark, the headlight of a coming Engine.

A TRIP TO THE SKIES.

It is a great blaze, but you cannot tell exactly how many inches it is across, for you can discover no disk; it is simply a blaze. So of these far off stars when seen through a telescope.

Orion has seven suns of vast magnitude revolving around each other in one grand whole. Who bounds their orbits? Who keeps this vast cluster of orbs in motion? What "bands" encircle this whole—this Orionis?

Finite mortals may well represent themselves as "dust and ashes" in the presence of Him who alone can "loose the bands of Orion." In this whole, beams forth the seven prismatic colors, in the rainbow light of God's myriad worlds, balanced and held in Heaven's glorious arc, notwithstanding Job and Abraham and John and Stephen have disappeared from the world of matter, and dust has returned to dust. Still the great question remains unanswered by any king or potentate, none can say "I can loose the bands of Orion;" I can take out of this whole, one sun; I can break these bands whenever I please."

Whoever discovers the majesty of God's works, will not be likely to make him like to mortals—fickle, frail, transient. "Thou thoughtest I was altogether such a one as thyself,"—Ps. 50-21, only applies to those who love to dwell in pitiable darkness. "The Heavens declare the glory of God and the firmament showeth His handiwork."

Orion is one of the grandest of the celestial groups, and here let our chariot of thought wait with patience the will of our great and grand Master, and ask ourselves, are we the children of the Highest, and are these starry skies to be the home of the saints of all ages?

Our next journey will be to the constellation of Taurus, to visit that beautiful group, the Seven Sisters—Pleiades.

CHAPTER VIII.

ORION.

We are now stopping at Orionis—Orion—called Orionis because there are many orbs, all rolling around each other in this grand whole. The outline of Orion is marked by a parallelogram of four great Suns. Betelgeuse is a red star of great beauty and brilliancy—a star of the first magnitude, and with Bellatrix, Saiph and Rigel, form a beautiful triangle, which is indeed, only a climax or vertex of another triangle composed of stars, of which Betelgeuse is one of the most brilliant. Thus we see that this noted and radiant star, represents a point in both the parallelogram and the triangle of Orionis. Then only a little distance off and near the centre of this parallelogram, are a cluster of stars, supposed to form the outlines of the belt of Orion, or the "bands of Orion."—Job, 38-31. These bands appear double; one, in the appearance of burnished silver, and still farther out and aloof from the silver belt, is another broad belt, like unto burnished gold. These double bands were referred to of God, as marvelous wonders, and Job invited to investigate, if he considered himself as equal to God in astronomical knowledge. "Cans't thou loose the bands of Orion?"

The constellation of Orion is represented by a furious hunter, with a club in his hand, madly engaged in conflict with Tarsus—the Bull—in whose breast the beautiful Pleiades is found. If the reader will, on or about the 10th of January, look directly overhead, he will obtain a grand view of Orion. That very bright star almost vertical, is in the right arm of the hero, midway between the armpit and the elbow; then follow off to the left a few degrees, and you will see three stars of the second magnitude; these are in the cheek of the hunter. One of these stars forms the point of the parallelogram. Then turn your atttention ten degrees south, and you will see a cluster of four stars; these are in the left foot of Orion, as it is raised to crush the head of Lupus. Then parallel with the first line down, a few degrees back, you see a bright yellow star in the thigh of the mighty hero, and parallel the same distance south, and you obtain the bounds of the parallelogram. About midway up the giant's body, are seen the rolling, burning suns above mentioned.

In the left limb of Orion, a little above the knee, you will discover the stars commonly known by the name of "Yard and Ell." It is supposed to mean a Flemish yard, which is three-quarters of one of our yards, and an English Ell, which is five quarters of a yard. The yard is of vast importance in measuring distances across the Heavens, for each of the three stars composing the Ell, are just three degrees apart, and by retaining these distances in the eye, the student can easily ascertain all distances on the planisphere of the heavens.

Now please look a moment at the "Yard and Ell;" catch the distance in the eye, (three degrees apart) and then we will journey on, thanking Orion for the yard stick by which we can measure distances from one star to another without astronomical aparatus.

It is millions of miles on a tangent line southeast across the Earth's elliptic from the brilliant suns in the face of Orion, to the mighty cluster between the horns of Tarsus. But millions of miles in our chariot, is not more than a few rods on a railway train, so we can soon climb up to view the brilliancies of suns in gorgeous colors, for where double triple, quadruple or septuple stars are found, all the seven prismatic colors can be seen. On this account the grandeur of Orion is incomprehensible. But the Heavens are full of wonders, and our eternity of being is only adequate to the mighty research.

In passing onward to meet the mighty Taurus, whose horns are exceedingly high and whose ferocious appearance we should think would daunt the heroic Orion, we are greatly astonished to know that in the head of this monster Bull—Taurus—is Aldebaran, the star of all stars; the great center around which, many of our astronomers believe, all the systems in our astronomical universe radiates. If so here is the centre of one hundred and seventeen million systems, and our solar system perhaps the least of all. These masses of worlds, these associations of planets, are all in motion around our present point of observation, and even this great centre is in ceaseless motion.

Let us step aboard our train of thought and visit the wonderful Aldebaran, and contemplate the majesty of this mighty centre. Now if our solar system revolves around this central star, it requires, at the terrible speed of 86,000 miles per second, (the speed that light travels) the long, long period of eighteen million years to complete a single revolution. Is there not a beauty, majesty and grandeur in the contemplation of the "glory of the stars?"

Could we for a moment realize this grandeur, this beauty, and associate ourselves with God as our Father and the heavens as our celestial mansion through Christ, the great Redeemer, how cheering it would make the study of astronomy!

CHAPTER IX.

Aldebaran.

If the majesty of mind is to be found in the ennobling contemplation of the magnitudes and motions, the brilliancy of colors and the handiwork of God as our Father in the systems and galaxies of the heavens, how dark must have been the age when mythology had its triumph! Then the height of intellectual imagination is recorded as follows:

"Orion was a famous hunter. Becoming enamored of Merope, he desired to marry her. Œnopion, her father, opposing the choice, took a favorable opportunity, and put out the eyes of the unwelcome suitor. The blinded hero followed the sound of Cyclop's hammer until he came to Vulcan's forge. He, taking pity, instructed Kedalion to conduct him to the abode of the sun.

"Placing his guide on his shoulder, Orion proceeded to the east, and, at a favorable place,

'Climbing up a narrow gorge, fixed his blank eyes upon the sun.'

"The healing beams restored him to sight.

"As a punishment for having profanely boasted that he was able to conquer any animal the earth could produce, he was bitten in the heel by a scorpion. Afterward, Diana placed him among the stars, where Sirius and Brocyon, his dogs, follow him, the Pleiades fly before him, and far remote is the Scorpion by whose bite he perished."

We need only in contrast to quote,

"Cans't thou loose the bands of Orion?" Job, 38-31.

How cheering to realize that the next race above us—the angels—are the managers of these ceaseless activities, and that so perfect is their mechanical skill that no earthly time-piece can be more exact, and though change is rung out on every peal of earthly progress, yet the stars appear and fail not; they hurry on but do not collide.

Here we can behold the myriad Cherubim of the skies, giving glory to God in the activities of life force, while they manage these material magnitudes, and if a convoy of angels are commissioned to visit this mundane orb for the instruction or relief of God's beloved children, they with instant flight reach our shores and sometimes say: "O, Daniel, a man greatly beloved, understand the words that I speak unto thee and stand upright, for unto thee am I sent," and then with equal fleetness leave us and are gone. Who but these, govern these mighty fleets of stars that twinkle in their distant glory? Who?

At Aldebaran, we can behold the greatest activities that we have ever beheld since we left the many mansions of Glory.

Just to think of this vastness of worlds which astronomers have calculated! Of course, exactness of count could hardly be expected, yet they, with their means and methods of astronomical exactness, can arrive at conclusions with so much certainty as to announce such stupendous centers.

Dr. J. G. Steele remarks in reference to the appearance of the sidereal skies as follows:

"Could we cross the Gulf of space beyond Neptune, the stars now so familiar to us would look strangely enough in their new groupings. As one, in riding through a forest, sees the trees apparently increase in size and open up to view before him, while they decrease in size and close up behind him, forming clusters and groups which constantly change as he is passing along; so as our earth travels with the solar system on its immense sidereal journey, the stars will grow larger and brighter in front, while those behind us will appear smaller and dimmer. Since in addition to this, the stars themselves are in motion, with varying velocity and in different directions, the constellations must change still more rapidly; so, as ultimately to transform entirely the appearance of the heavens. In time the 'Bands of Orion' will be loosened and the 'Seven Sisters' will glide apart into remote space. Such are the distances, however, that, although these movements have been going on constantly, yet, since the creation of man no variation has occurred that is perceptable, save to the watchful astronomer. Nothing in nature is as invariable as the stars. They are the standards of time. Myriads of years must elapse before new star maps will be required."

Looking from Aldebaran, we see away yonder in the constellation of the Swan, a star which seems to be a cluster center. It is 61-Cygnia. Is it a single, double or quadruple star? It is to us perhaps the nearest cluster centre. Now behold it in its full blaze; it is a double star, and is, with all its surroundings, moving through space at the incomprehensible velocity of 86,000 miles per second. How vast its magnitude! The diameter across this double star is not less than three billions of miles—it is larger than the orbit of our vast solar system and more than five hundred billions of miles away. Who can comprehend the majesty and glory of this double star?

Here the glorified of God's angels superintend the motions of this vast whole, in harmony with His will who bounds and fills and equals all.

Let us look again away, away to the constellation of Lyra—the Harp. There in brilliant splendor shines in ceaseless glory the planet Vega, which we might have mistaken for a single star; but to our astonishment it is a binary (double) star, and a double binary. One great sun revolving around another great sun, and these revolving around the others in one vast blaze. Four great suns in one flame of incandescent burning hydrogen with a brilliancy equal to twelve thousand of such suns as the sun that apparently rises and sets every twenty-four hours—our sun.

Here is a cluster center, around which groups of systems of thousands of revolving stars are radiating in harmony of motion incomprehensibly grand!

Now, this cluster center is undoubtedly one of the 117,000,000 fleets of stars throughout the via Lactea of our starry universe, as we gaze upon it from Aldebaran.

We are now in the constellation of Taurus, and as the "Seven Sisters"—"Seven Stars"—Pleiades, is only a short distance away, and in the same constellation, we will allow Orion to confront Taurus with his huge club, while we rest from our journeying, and then we will visit Pleiades.

"Canst thou bind the sweet influences of Pleiades?"—Job 38-31.

CHAPTER X.

ALCYONE.

Who formed these nebulæ, wondrous skies,
Where twinkling gems in glory rise.
                My Father.
Who bids me look for glory, where,
And says my future home is there.
                My Father.
Who spans the heavens, who fills the sky,
From Nadir up to Zenith high.
                My Father.
Who in the skies prepares a home,
And bids his earth-born children come.
                My Father.
In rapturous thought who bids me look,
And read my name in life's fair book.
                My Father.
O blessed home, O sweet abode,
O may I share thy love, O God,
                My Father.

Aldebaran is a fiery red star of the first magnitude and is really the right eye of Tarus; and is it not a most venerable eye. We should hardly think Orion could ever expect to put out the Bull's eye, even though he holds a mighty club.

It might be well for us now at so vast a center, to scan well the heavens in every direction.

There are many readers of this Trip to the Skies, who have read of the beautiful maiden, chained to a rock for her determined virtue, and how she was rescued by her lover just as the sea monster had opened his mouth to destroy her —Andromeda. There are incomprehensible wonders connected with this constellation, and it matters but little to us as to the myth of ancient Greece, or whether Andromeda was saved by Perseus or Orion, or whether the chain that held her to the rock had gold or silver links, or whether Perseus actually possessed Pluto's helmet, which rendered him invisible to the serpent he destroyed; nor will we weep with the parents of Andromeda, as they saw the huge serpent open his mouth to swallow up their child, while they were powerless to render any aid; nor shall we shout when Perseus brings down his glittering sword and severs the serpent's head from his body. No. This mythology we take for what it is worth, but the constellation of Andromeda is still in the northern heavens, and looking through the eye of Taurus, we can get a glimpse of the majesty of the heavens by the survey of this constellation.

Lest some of our readers think we draw largely from fiction and imagination in our "Trip," let me call your attention to the remarks of Prof. Bond, of the Cambridge observatory. But first please remember that all nebulæ (clusters of stars) are divided into six classes, viz: Elliptic, Annular, Spiral, Planetery, Irregular Nebulæ and Nebulous stars.

The first, the Elliptic, are the most abundant of any in the heavens. Under this classification Andromeda, more than a thousand years ago, became one of the greatest and is indeed visible to the naked eye. Prof. Bond remarks:

"If we suppose this nebulæ to be one continuous bed of stars, of different sizes for its entire extent, it must comprise the enormous number of thirty millions."

Says Dr. Steele: "The distance of such nebulæ from the earth entirely passes our comprehension. Some astronomers have estimated that a ray of light requires 800,000 years to span the gulf that intervenes. Imagination wearies itself in the attempt to understand these figures. They only teach us some of the limitless expanses of that space in which God is working out the mysterious problem of creation."

It is indeed an easy matter to write down a whole column of figures and to comprehend this vastness of numerals would be simply impossible, but if we are immortal beings I care not how long the colums of numerals may be, you and I will live to hear the last year's record called off, whether it be 30 or 300 millions of years hence. So vast is life.

There have as yet been but four annular nebulæ discovered. These are in the form of a ring. Lyra, the Harp, has one, first seen by Herschel, and having a central nebulæ, much after the appearance of a hoop over which a piece of gauze was suspended. As seen through Lord Ross' great telescope, the filmy parts of the nebulæ are real twinkling stars, which if no further from the earth than 61-Cygnia, the diameter of each must be at least two thousand million miles. It is very probable that the nebulæ stars far exceed this distance. Then if we continue to survey the skies in reference to "spiral" nebulæ, we shall find the most brilliant in ·Canes Venatici. If any one has ever seen the spiral antics, as shown in our holiday fireworks, they can faintly conceive of a heavenly display as is apparent through astronomical telescopes. "It consists of brilliant spirals, sweeping outward from a central neucleus, and all overspread with a multitude of stars."

"Irregular nebulæ" are those that can have no definite shape or form. Some writers liken them to broken clouds of every possible form. There is one of these near our present outlook in the southern horn of Taurus, another in the sword handle of Orion.

Well did the Psalmist observe, "the heavens declare the glory of God," especially if we look at these singular nebulæ as seen through the telescope, their measureless distance from us—Centauri, for instance, placed at 42,800,000,000 of miles away. Writes a great astronomer:

"But owing to the almost infinite depth of the abyss of the heavens at which these nebulæ exist, thousands of years, perhaps thousands of centuries would be necessary to reveal any perceptible movement." (Guillemin.)

Let us now leave Aldebaran and pass on a few millions of miles triangularly across the Earth's orbit as seen on the planisphere of the heavens and we are among the "sweet influences of Pleiades."

Many thousand years ago the "sweet influences" of these seven stars threw their rays of light across the track of the patient Job, and perhaps he, like ourselves, beheld only the light of these stellar orbs without the knowledge of any "influence" at all, permeating, controlling and regulating vast systems throughout the high arch of heaven. It would seem that since these stars have been seen and counted, one of the number has stepped down and out, leaving at present only six that are visible to the naked eye; but tradition informs us that there were originally seven. One of the principal stars of this constellation is Alcyone, which has been considered by many the great grand center of the milky way. Whether this opinion originated from the word "influences," or from actual astronomical phenomena we are unable to say. It is a fact unquestionable, that Alcyone is a mighty star, and by some strange affinity the Pleiades are associative, and in harmony revolve around some common center, or other systems revolve around Alcyone. These lights in the heavens are so far away that their distances from each other may indeed be vast, while to us they seem to be in immediate proximity. Still the question of the Almighty, "canst thou bind the sweet influences of Pleiades" is important. He that knew acknowledged an influence far out in its attractive power—an influence that He alone could "bind"—an influence genial, generous, "sweet," all-pervading, all-affecting, all-controlling.

If so it must be that Aldebaran is not the central orb of the heavenly galaxy, but Alcyone. Prof. Maudler, of Prussia, arrived at the conclusion, after careful study and by the aid of every conceivable appliance, that the science of astronomy has at its command that Alcyone is the grand nebulæ center and that Pleiades has this honor. Be this as it may, let us visit Alcyone. But some one will ask how large across is this mighty star, and how far away. Figures will do us no good in this matter of distances. It is supposed to be not less than five thousand three hundred and eighty billion, two thousand million of miles away, and Prof. Maudler thinks it would take a ray of light with its awful fleetness 537 years to reach us.

These masses of worlds, these associations of planets, are all in motion around our present post of observation, at least the constellation of Taurus carries off the prize either in Aldebaran or in Alcyone, and we think the testimony from a biblical standpoint favors Pleiades—Alcyone. If a glass could be discovered that would give us a disk instead of a blaze we might readily measure the diameter of any or all the heavenly orbs; but such is not attainable, hence diameters are all guess work where a disk does not obtain.

Can we possibly feel at home so far away as Alcyone, and after a little rest pass on to the southern skies and behold the emblem cross of redemption with stars of various colors, like as Herschel remarks, "a brilliant casket of jewels" standing in the heavens, the admiration of the cherubic legions of glory? We will try.

CHAPTER XI.

ALCYONE.

O glorious arch of heaven,
        Display celestial;
The golden gates away--
From things terrestrial,
Begotten God, of Thee--
Beyond our sphere of thought,
Twinkling in joyous glee,
        Still not forgot.

Ah! See the mighty cross—
        Exalted high,
With rainbow glory,
O'er its southern sky,
        What twinkling gems,
        How bright they shine.
        It's glory's shrine
Seraph behold, it's thine,
        and mine,
T'adore the Sacrifice Divine.

We were stopping at Alcyone, in the Constellation of Pleiades, gazing in awe at the heavenly spiral display of Canes Venatici, which so overwhelmed us that we begged for rest; but now let us proceed.

We are so accustomed to look at the stars and constellations of the northern circumpolar skies, that to be interested in an investigation of the unseen of the southern, may require a more extended journey than we wish to undertake; still we believe our readers will journey with us, away across the "star-spangled" vault, that thereby they may obtain a wider scope of knowledge than it is possible to attain from actual observation, which few, indeed, have time and means necessary to such an undertaking. Some half century ago, Bessell, the great astronomer, undertook the herculean task of arraying the southern stellar orbs in a catalogue of positions and magnitudes. His field included all the stars between 45 degrees north declination and 15 degrees south, and down to the ninth magnitude.

In this arrangement he included all stars to one-fifteenth the brightness of those beheld by natural vision.

Prof. Bessell carried on this great and successful survey of the Southern Heavens from the year 1821 to 1833, in which he made 72,000 observations, locating 62,380 stars of different magnitudes.

Since then, these have been carefully compiled and their catalogues published by the Observatory Imperial of Russia. These observations have been of incalculable value to modern Astronomers.

Near the close of the last century, La Lande, a

French astronomer, undertook to locate all the stars between the north pole—Polaris—and the southern tropic, making for this purpose 47,000 observations. These were computed and published at the expense of the British Government, but the superiority of the instruments of modern times rendered the labors of Prof. Bessell essentially more important.

Prof. Argelander, who gained his popularity from Prof. Bessell's instruction, made a more thorough exploration of the stellar skies as "zone" observations.

In the circumpolar he included from 45 degrees north to 80, and from 15 to 31 degrees south; in all, about 50,000 observations, overcoming difficulties that had totally discouraged other astronomers.

Gilliss, of our own country, made many valuable discoveries at Chili, and it has been hoped that his observations, embracing a series of zones, would be published by our government, notwithstanding the decease of the great astronomer.

About 1860, the English astronomer, Prof. Carrington, explored to the tenth degree from the north pole.

Thus far, from 30 degrees south of the equator to the north pole has the heavens received the greater portion of all astronomical observations.

Difficulties insurmountable have until recently hedged up the way towards a complete survey of the southern skies, and these are by far the grandest of the heavens.

Navigators have, for a quarter of a century, remarked upon the grandeur and beauty of the surroundings of the south pole; but no nation has seemed at all interested in its grand survey, and from ship-board a meager observation only could be taken. As early as the beginning of the sixteenth century, navigators discovered brilliantly illuminated patches of what seemed to be clouds, and named them "Magellanic clouds," as well as others of dense blackness, called "coal sacks."

Dr. B. A. Gould, from his observations in Cordova, Argetine Republic, remarks of the grandeur of the southern constellations, "The glory of the southern sky near the Cross is indescribable. There, where the Milky Way is crossed by the thick stream of bright stars, which skirt this river of light its brilliancy is wonderfully increased, and it exhibits a magnificence unequaled in any other portion of the heavens."

And now reader, we at Alcyone are ten degrees north of the equator, and from hence to the constellation of the Cross, near the southern pole, is a vast, vast journey, and the perils, of such a trip remind us of the crossing of the river of death. Through this chilly stream we all must pass, and happy shall we be, if—

> "On the Cross uplifted high,
> Where the Saviour deigned to die."

we are permitted to behold our blessed Lord, as a "Lamb slain from the foundation of the world,"

We, in our fleet journey across the heavens, will pass so many grand and magnificent equatorial constellations that should receive more than a passing notice, that we hardly know as it is best to pass silently by these wonders.

Some conception of the vastness of our journey across the heavens may be obtained by a remembrance of the computed distance from the Earth to the Constellation Centaur, which is nearest to the brilliant Cross, and which is represented by the vastly overwhelming numerals of 42,800,000,000 of miles away.

Then, to take into consideration our distance at Alcyone from the earth we inhabit, we are lost in the vast abyss of space, which seems, indeed, boundless.

In order to successfully reach our destination

(the Southern Cross and Altar), we had better follow the earth's orbit from east to west, a few million of miles, until we arrive at the Solstitial Colure, and then follow that line across the heavens to the South Pole, as a direct line is the nearest path from one object to another.

Tejat, a grand and brilliant star, welcomes us as we reach the intersections of the earth's orbit and the Solstitial Colure. A little further on and you discover the constellation Gemini, or the Twins; but we are on a southern trip, and cannot stop to inquire as to the mythology of Castor or Pollux. Here we pass Betelguese, a brilliant star in the right arm of Orion, whose grandeur we have previously contemplated.

And now we have crossed the great equatorial line of the heavens. That constellation on our left is Lepus—the Hare; the one on our right, Canis Major—the Greater Dog.

We are now passing the beak of Columbia Noachi—Noah's Dove. Ah! the olive branch is a brilliant cluster of stars, that no doubt shone out on the deep flood of waters as brilliantly then as now. Here we pass the Telescopian, a constellation that represents the telescope with which Herschel surveyed the heavens. That grand constellation of stars a little to our right and in front of us is distinguished by the name of Peacock, and when covered with the Magellanic Clouds, exhibits a grandeur and glory faintly conceived of by those who have never made astronomy their study; and here is the Ara—the Altar from which the Magellanic Clouds constantly develop the Holy burning incense, that, as a sweet odor, vivifies the distant Cross, near the equinoxial Colure.

Just above the Altar you will discover two vastly bright stars, revolving around each other, covered as by a rainbow of incandescent light from the Magellanic Clouds, that devolop the uprush of continued incense, reaching far out towards the Starry Cross; and there is no night there, for these perpetually evolve an undiminishable glory far exceeding the brightness of 10,000 suns.

How strange that the heavens should so symbolize the Jewish Altar as found in the temple of God, whose "Shekinah" never ceased in its burning, as of incense before the throne of the God of Abraham and of Israel. And can there be coal-black clouds between the Altar and the Cross? Can these brilliant skies be darkened by Pernigram Clouds—"Coal Sacks," as mariners call them—Anthracinus Clouds. So it appears near this constellation.

We will stop at Beta, in the Constellation of the Altar, amid the perpetual brilliancy of light that surrounds it, and humbly kneel in adoration and wonder, and place upon this hallowed symbol our incense of holy devotion to the Father of Spirits, whose children we are, and whose hand has led us far out to behold the matchless wonders of the skies.

CHAPTER XII.

To the Altar.

If we proceed from the constellation of Hadley's Quadrant at the South Pole, and travel along the Solstitial colure ninety degrees, we shall reach the Southern Altar—our last resting place.

Now look abroad and grasp the skies in this almost unexplored region. From the South Pole at right angles with the Solstitial Colure and ninety degrees along the Equatorial Colure, you will easily discover the Southern Cross, being nearly a triangle of distances—Pole, Altar and Cross.

Having stopped at the Altar to pay our adorations to Deity, let us as His children arise and behold our Father's glory bedecked symbol, which no genius less than the Supreme Architect of the skies could devise and so grandly adorn.

Alpha, Beta and Gamma, three brilliant stars, stretch a perfect line over our heads, around which and continuous with said line of stars, is a rainbow wreath in heaven's prismatic colors beautifully entertwined. Below the central star of this wreath are two brilliant stars in ceaseless rotation around each other, fringed with spiral phenomena, and reducing the Magelaine flame to a pot of incense, flowing away toward the Cross in continuous elliptical grandeur.

Were this single wreath of star-decked glory all we behold of the Altar of stars, we could say—

"Enough, my gracious Lord,
Let faith triumphant cry;
My soul can on this promise rest,
My (senses) on it die"—

but this is only a small part of the wonders of the Altar.

This stellar emblem has a cornice of stars, so to speak, surrrounding it, and forming a brilliant purple flame, from which a gauze-like scintillation reveals the four sides of the Altar resting upon a pillar of stars, every star appearing in sublime imitation of the description given by the Revelator of the foundation stone of the new Jerusalem. (See Rev. 11: 19-21.)

In gazing at this, the telescopic observer is lost in the indescribable wonder of the southern skies, and steps back, like Herschel, with an "Oh! wonderful casket of jewels! indescribable glory! marvelous wonders of the skies!" etc. Had we in our possession the southern portion of South America, on which we could in safety erect a telescopic tower, our observations need not be so clothed with amazement; but from ship-board view, it is wonderful that the old ocean would cease her motion so long as to catch the glimpses of glory so grandly unfolded by astronomers.

The seven prismatic colors, viz., red, blue, orange, yellow, indigo, green, and violet, are, in this constellation, so brilliantly decorative, that no artist can imitate these wonders, as they are really indescribable. It surpasses the skill of any master of the fine or decorative arts in its grandeur and in its glory.

We almost wonder if this is not the grand telephone office from whence the ceaseless prayers of the saints are repeated in the ear of the Lord of Sabbaoth, and from whom we catch the answer in the known voice of the Master, "A stranger will they not follow, for they know not the voice of strangers?" Surely, if there is a symbol of vast import, it must be the Altar; for upon that hallowed place the hosts of the millions redeemed by grace have laid their every sacrifice, and should not Deity honor with indescribable glory a symbol so radiant with pardon, peace, and joy?

Some people look at the stars as they do at an apple tree full of delicious fruit. Ah! the fruit is all; the Creator's glory, nothing. To such persons "Our Trip" is a meaningless fable; but to Christians, and here let me explain my meaning of the word "Christians": *Those who see in God a Father, and grasp the idea of a child's rights amidst the starry constellations of heaven.* To such, "Our Trip" will be a welcome prelibation of the coming glory of the great God.

If this starry Altar is not the grand telephonic center from whence the prayers of the saints commingle in celestial harmonies, where can there be found another center so grand in all heaven's high pavillions; from whence, if stripped of all malevolence, hypocrisy, doubt, or deception, the inner soul, sinking into the eternal changeless, can grasp the glory of God's grand symbol, the starry Altar. As the drowning man grasps the outflung rope, hardly aware which is safety, the rope, or the vessel, or the mighty seamen who are dragging him on board, so we, gazing at this wonderful "Casket of Jewels," can only with adoration exclaim, the Master is calling from labor to refreshment.

The grandeur of this constellation is vastly augmented by a careful survey of its decorations—the millions of star-gems surrounding it, of exceeding beauty and brilliancy. It is, indeed, one of the few constellations of the heavens that at all resembles the prototype from which the constellation is named; and this is so perfect that thousands of thousands who had any just conceptions of an altar would almost intuitively exclaim, "The Altar! see the Altar!" Stars of every color, so artistically blended, flood its walls on every side, and embellish and illuminate its exceeding altitude to such an extent that language fails to give only the faintest conception of the reality. It is, indeed, the star-adorned Altar of the Most High, whose thoughts of grandeur so far exceed ours as do his ways in the unexplored heavens exceed those of his earth-begotten children, who, with amazement and wonder, often exclaim, "Can the teachings of Astronomy be a reality—a fact?"

Let us now climb up from star to star, from gem to gem, from jewel to jewel, until we can, from its towering height, observe clearly the blended rainbow hues of its symbolic incense, and gazing far across the heavens, catch the form of the Cross, and the direction we must take to reach it, and haste to that grandest of all which is grand in the heavens—the Cross of Redemption. And now, fellow-travelers, let us enter the current of incense in our train of thought, leaving upon the Altar our oblations and thank offerings, and hasten across the unknown to the emblem cross of the stars.

Away yonder is the constellation named Centaur—a beast and man united; the archer and the lion; a very strange and meaningless chimera of some disturbed imagination; but they had to name it something, so they called it Centaur. That one a little further on is called the King's Oak; but yonder see the starry Cross of Redemption.

It seems to be so far across this triangle, and such an unexplored wilderness of unnamed stars and constellations before us, that the imagination itself tires of the survey. But look! Yonder rises a "Coal Sack," an anthracinus cloud of densest darkness, of blackness, so awful, that we, like Moses at Sinai, are compelled to say, "I exceedingly fear and quake." It hastens across the heavens, and we cannot escape its gloom. Now, the seething fury of darkness is upon us; its rolling billows dash in frightful blackness in our faces; and dismay, without a pole star, compass, or ray of light to lift at all the gloom, is upon us.

We were once, as our guide informed us, three

miles from daylight in the great Mammoth Cave of Kentucky, and he had all our lights extinguished, so that we might sense the darkness, so terrible, so exceedingly black; there the friction match would light again our lamps, but not here. Whirling, sinking, rising; all is dark and black; no Altar in sight now—no crown, no cross; lost! lost! lost! Did you ever reflect on Gethsemane, where an Altar of sacrifice was occupied by a single victim, "sweating, as it were, great drops of blood," and how, on a subsequent day, the same victim upon the cross was visited by this dense anthracinus cloud? There was no eclipse of the sun then, and philosophy could not explain the phenomenon. "It was dark from the sixth to the ninth hour," and then this anthracinus cloud returned to its native sky. But did you ever reflect that the agony in that darkness was intense? Forsaken, neglected, lost! "Eloi, Eloi, lama sabacthani?" We now pass through, as all must who approach the Cross, this black cloud of darkened vision: "eyes, but cannot see; cannot see the kingdom of God."

So now in our "Trip" all is dark, all is blackness, all is peril. Our train has no track—our ship has no helm—our engine has no engineer. Black chaos: "outer darkness" presides with awful aspect; boundless nothingness surrounds us on every side. Oh! how we need a guide—a deliverer—a Saviour. Ah, look! the Cross appears; the blackness has passed. We are approaching the wonder of wonders—the Starry Cross.

The Southern Cross we believe to be God's grand symbol upon a scale somewhat commensurate with the purposes of eternal redemption, originating before the world was, and unfolding the seven attributes of God as a sublimely developed whole, showing Himself to be a God of infinite mercy. No mind can fathom the depth of this celestial labyrinth, or say to him that formed it, why hast thou fashioned it thus? As visitors, we can survey this starry wonder, and content ourselves by remembering that Cherubim and Seraphim, angels of might and power, may view this prototypic cross as heaven's great and grand symbol, and not as a few feet of a transverse wooden shaft. We shall endeavor to describe this "Casket of Jewels" erected of God (as seen in the southern skies) as the honored symbol of the sacrifice of the great Messiah—the wondrous prototypic cross of human redemption. We wish our readers also to remember that the southern Magellanic clouds of incandescent light visited once the hills of Judea on the night of the grand transfiguration of the Messiah—"a bright cloud overshadowed them"—and then it returned to its native sky, where, when human redemption ceases, the Starry Cross will forever glitter with its celestial scintillations.

CHAPTER XIII.

The Starry Cross.

HOME.

And, Father, is that realm of light
  Our dear eternal home?
Hast thou redeemed us through thy might?
  Wilt thou say, "Children, come?"
Our finite minds would grasp the power—
  Thine all-creating word—
That throws aside this shadowy hour,
  And brings us near to God.
Then haste these darkened clouds away,
  Let brighter clouds arise,
Till we behold eternal day
  Amidst celestial skies.

We had just emerged from the blackness of that terrible anthracinus cloud, "Coal Sack," of the southern skies, and had caught the form of the Starry Cross; but we had neglected to locate the constellation of the Bird of Paradise or the Crown of Glory. These constellations are very beautiful, and are to our right as we pass in a triangular line from the Altar of the Cross.

On, with the velocity of thought, our train is passing objects that at first appear as fire-specks afar off, but now appear in grand proportions, and their majesty astonishes us greatly. Now, reader, stop and reflect a moment in reference to the probable character of the great God. There must be in his works some manifestations infinitely more grand than others; and it would be natural to suppose that, in some of His works, His declarative glory might far excel those of minor creations. And, then, if a "Son is given" as an offering of God for the salvation of man, what should the heavens declare as co-eternal with such a sacrifice? Such a gift, so great, so grand, is the gift of God's only begotten Son. It is almost a law of nations to erect monuments of exceeding grandeur to those who have achieved the greatest type of magnanimity and devotion to the rulers they have served. And whoever suffered for others, "the just for the unjust," that he might develop one attribute of God, that in no other way could possibly be unfolded but by this sacrifice—the Christ of God. How could Mercy be revealed without an object, and of what value is an undeveloped attribute? God possesses seven attributes. Six of these need no negative: Light, Life, Justice, Love, Truth and Holiness need no association by which a necessity arises for a negative to co-exist; but Mercy must remain eternally concealed without a negative.

The plan of human pro-creation, in which the seven senses constitute the man mortal, and the seven attributes which constitute the man spiritual, with liability to a separation and decomposition of the mortal, involved in itself the development of God's attribute—Mercy—salvation from the condemnation of transgression through a Messiah. If, then, the mightiest of the mighty made the greatest of all sacrifices, surely the monument, the emblem of this sacrifice, must outreach, in glory, all others.

We are now far past the utmost view of our little world; and on we haste with the velocity of thought towards the grand object of our journey. But look! What is that "sea of glass," that vast plane of crystal rock, before us? Ah! it is the Rock of Ages—the base upon which rests the Starry Cross. How exceedingly broad, how beautifully commingled with the loveliest colors the mind can grasp. This wonderful Rock is pure carbon, like brilliant diamonds, mingled with all the transparencies of quartz in every hue and color. Our finite conception can in no possible way measure the length or the breadth of the Rock of Ages. Here let us rest our train of thought and contemplate the vastness of our surroundings and the glory of the southern skies; for here, more than at any other place, "the heavens declare the glory of God." Our earth is vastly out of sight, while other wonders multiply in strange proportion. Well did the Revelator, John, call this Rock "a sea of glass, mingled with fire." To us it is a vast and beautiful plain of inwrought gems of sparkling glory. From hence rises the wonderful cross that far excels our highest conceptions of grandeur and display. The breadth of the upright shaft exceeds the diameter of the earth's orbit, and the heavens declare its glory; and the majesty of the suns composing it transcends the majesty of thought itself. It is not composed of a few rolling orbs, but of millions. High up they rise toward the eternal gates of glory in the splendor of "network, lily-work, and pomegranite," until we behold the upright shaft of the Cross as a cluster of jewels, and of all colors beautifully blended. Those two immense shafts of diamond rock that are beside the Cross of Stars and so exceedingly high, represent "strength and beauty," and are wonderfully cleft asunder from top to bottom, exhibiting, in their beauty of colors, the rose of Sharon.

"Rock of Ages, cleft for me;
Let me hide myself in Thee."

If we bring our telescope to aid us in looking upon and along the line of the Cross, we shall easily see the blood-red stars that tell of Him who was "bruised for our transgressions," especially the star representing the pierced side of the Adorable; and on a closer observation we shall be more than astonished to behold—

"A fountain filled with blood,
Drawn from Immanuel's veins"—

opened for sin and uncleanliness, outflowing from the foot of the Cross of Redemption. Could it be otherwise than that the eternal God, who possesses all power, all glory, all might, and whose love transcends, so to speak, His eternity? Could it be otherwise than that such an emblem as this must eternally appear in the heavens, when we take into consideration the fact that "God's love to His Son was infinitely intense, and that he had promised to glorify His name above all other names—"the glory I had with thee before the world was?" Oh! wonderful Rock of Ages, inseparable with jewels and gems in the angelic regions of eternity. And is this heaven? No, indeed; it is heaven's great dial of a single dispensation—that of grace. Time will pass away; but, like the pyramids of Egypt, these shafts of stars will remain as an anchor to the soul forever and ever. If we look abroad, as now we may, over this transparent diamond sea, we shall behold an endless array of arbors, most exquisitely decorated with gems of translucent splendor and trees bearing heaven's own fruit and foliage; and a host of angels, all in delight at our meeting, and joining with us, as in Judea, in our songs of "peace on earth and good will to men." God has not left this Rock tenantless, nor the emblem of sacrifice unguarded; and while we look up we can sing—

> "Burst, ye emerald gates, and bring
> To my raptured vision,
> All the ecstatic joys that spring
> Round this bright elysian."

The Mirage.

Here is, indeed, the *mirage* of Redemption, reflected back from the throne of God and the Lamb—"a lamb slain from the foundation of the world."

Through this reflected grandeur we can see by faith a gauze-like form—a symbol Saviour—still extended upon the cross, and feel drawn from earth up to Him. "And I, if I be lifted up from the earth, will draw all men unto Me." So we are drawn by the blood of the crucified one.

We might ask if this form on the Starry Cross is the "real presence" of the Christ; and the mirage only will answer, Behold the great Creator's grand *symbol* of eternal redemption—Christ on the cross. And we might further ask, What suffered and died upon the cross so human as to leave this faith-seen form amidst these scintillations of the cross? Ah! it was the senses of Jesus, so holy, so pure, as to constitute the celestial mind of Christ to be for sin an offering. Like our senses—our mind, that sleeps in the wardrobe of Christ, to be worn as a spotless garment at the resurrection of the just—so of Jesus, only He was the resurrection and the life, and we are in Him.

Hence, we in this mirage—this symbol—may by faith behold Him; and looking, find life through His name.

It is in the world's great mind to worship an image—a Mediator. Some worship Mahomet as this mediator; some the Ganges; some the tombs of the saints; some Juggernaut; but still the idea of a mediator, present or to come, finds an echo in the world's great mind. This may all have originated from this one universal command, viz., "Look unto me, all ye ends of the earth, and be saved."

So, if we can, in this mirage, behold the "Son

of Man lifted up," as did Moses lift up the brazen serpent in the wilderness, we, too, can be saved through His grace.

This is man's adjuvant, and must so continue until the retribution of all things. The attributes of God in Christ withdrew at his death, leaving the pure—the holy—senses of Jesus a sacrifice for sin; a grand and holy sacrifice co-equal with man's great salvation. The symbol we here behold' "This is my body which I give for the life of the world," is the symbol of "the sleep in Jesus" so often referred to in the Scriptures; but we must not mistake this emblem for the real Christ. Some mistake the bread and wine in the Lord's last supper in the same manner. Hear Him: "I am in the Father, and the Father in Me." It is impossible, then, for a symbol to be the substance it represents. Here we behold, as did the children of Israel, the brazen serpent; and, although it was neither God nor a serpent, yet by looking at it health was restored; so of this human sacrifice, look and live.

Our Lord and Master, in reference to penalties, remarked that certain sins "hath never forgiveness in this world, or the world to come." This implies clemency even here, but no individual promise is made to any but those who believe. Here inside these brilliant walls do we not behold snowy white robes? This is the wardrobe of the guest chamber, and all these robes have been washed and made white in the blood of the Lamb.

They are the mental force, the mind, the seven senses of those that fell asleep in Jesus. The senses are invisible to themselves, but not to the attributes. The soul, through the seven attributes, can look upon the senses as do the senses upon the human body; they are the earthly white robe, pure and clean, ready for the coming of the bridegroom, but they are not the soul.

These are not living realities, but mental forms, and only assume life again at the resurrection, when "mortality is swallowed up of life."

This "Rock of Ages" is the Paradise of God for all believers—for all of the infant race, and for all of the translated ones. Here is the reception chamber for the church of the Most High, the glory-crowned summit of redemption; but yonder hangs the anthracinus cloud—the "Coal Sacks" of outer darkness—which evolve into black despair forever and ever.

Let us, then, glance again at the cleft rock, at the guest chamber, the wardrobe, the decorations, the Starry Cross, and the ten thousand times ten thousand happy ones in celestial arbors along the banks of the river of life, and then let us return to the dim starlight of modern astronomy, and what do we behold? Only this: the heavens are everywhere lit up with the glory of the stars.

In concluding our "Trip to the Skies," our readers will observe that we have closely followed astronomical discoveries and biblical allusions; not that we suppose the Bible to be an astronomical book, but in it is the truth, and no scientific discoverer can possibly unearth facts that God's great monitor overlooked.

Hence, the reader's attention has been called to consider the two cloudy pillars that accompanied the children of Israel through the waters of the Red Sea; the one a bright, shining cloud ("Magellanic"), and the other an anthracinus ("Coal Sack") cloud of intense darkness—one that had once spread its impenetrable gloom over all Egypt—"darkness that could be felt." Also, at the Mount of Transfiguration the one, and at the cross the other; and that these clouds have always been associative with God's revelations to man.

That it belongs to Christian astronomy to locate these clouds as they now appear near the Southern Cross and Altar. Since a "cloud received

Him out of their sight" (Acts 1: 9), both the "Magellanic" and "Coal Sack" have remained in the southern skies, a wonder to a world of astronomers; and until the day that the heavens shall be aglow with this Magellanic flame and "outer darkness" reign in the far-off abyss of eternal night, these clouds will to our telescopes be visible. The reader has also been reminded of the fact that "mighty angels" fill the skies with their activities, that they are not mere trumpet-horns of the Almighty, but that their labors are needed in the skies, and that to us they are the blessed spiritual messengers of the great God; that when he brought His only begotten Son into the world, he said: "And let all the angels of God worship Him;" so whom we worship they also worship, and with them the redeemed must enjoy ecstatic delight, whether gazing at the Starry Cross or at the New Jerusalem "coming down from God out of heaven." Hence, we can say: "Oh! death, where is thy sting? Oh! grave, where is thy victory?" when departing this life. A stormless realm of glory awaits our upward flight to the skies, if we only have confessed our allegiance to the God of angels and the God of glory.

Nor could we have gained this knowledge of

the skies had not some mind penetrated the "Bands of Orion," or the "sweet influences of Pleiades," other than astronomers. Thousands of years have passed away, and still these grand old constellations continue to grace the heavenly arch. How unlike the weak-minded teachings of mythology is the grand system of Christian astronomy, and the still higher beauty, as the apostle has asserted, "for unto the angels hath He not put in subjection the world to come whereof we speak?" (Hebrews 2: 15) as though to the true loyalty of heaven He had reserved a glory far transcending the glory even of angels.

The attention of the reader has been carefully, and we think logically, called to the chance management of a machine so vast as is the stellar skies, and to the intelligent management of this galaxy by the labors of the mighty angels. By the latter we may expect a continuance of these stellar regulators of "time and seasons, of days and years," in perpetual harmony, until the ultimate and proximate purposes of God are accomplished.

In passing over this trip, the reader will grasp the majesty of these ponderous orbs, with all their gigantic proportions, hastening through space at a rate exceeding that of the Minie rifle ball whirled on its flight by the greatest possible force, so terrible. Even Mercury passed us at the speed of 12,000 miles an hour—three and one-third miles per second. A world of the size of Mercury hurrying on with ceaseless activity at such a bewildering speed. We see a passenger train flying over the track at one mile a minute—one mile in sixty seconds—and then turn and see a world pass us at three and one-third miles in a single second, and we are lost in the terrible whirl of worlds.

And to realize the million of million of worlds in the vast expanse, the motions and magnitudes of which, in our fleet chariot, we could only partially explore, the regularity of their orbits, their vast ponderability, the why and wherefore of this mighty display, and then to suppose in the near future that we shall have aught to do with this grandeur—with this majesty of worlds overwhelming as we might suppose the intellect of a Gabriel; to suppose and believe that we shall awake to realize this glory ourselves, we of earthly origin, with powers of mind hardly sufficient to grasp the majesty of these wonders, is indeed beatific. And what must the Christian's crown of glory be if it shines as the stars in the firmament forever and ever?

CHAPTER XIV.

HOMEWARD.

Let our fleet train of thought now leave these "Chambers of the South," (Job, 9: 8.) this wonderful constellation in the far off stellar skies, and ask ourselves where, in this limitless field, shall we find the South Pole—the grand climax of the heavenly arch. Directions, distances, place or position, avail but little in this vastly incomprehensible field of limitless space, and if susceptible to the contemplation of our surroundings, how worthless must all human glory appear. Still we wish to know of the trackless depths of space and as we shortly must leave this life for a life among the stars, it really becomes our duty to explore the Creator's works as being the final abode of his earth-begotten royalty.

If our *wish* could be a compass, then our train might fly with the velocity of thought back towards the little orb of our nativity; content with having seen the Starry Cross and Altar in the Chambers of the South.

Says Dr. J. D. Steele in his "Fourteen Weeks

in Astronomy:" "At the Southern pole there is no conspicuous star, but the richness and number of the neighboring stars compensate this deficiency, and give to the heavens an incomparable splendor."

Here is the magnificent constellation Argo, in which we find Canopus looked upon in ancient times as next to Sirius in brilliancy. A variable star now surpasses it in brightness. Nearly at the height of the South pole blazes the

"Southern Cross."

There is no mythology from ancient Greece or Rome that attaches to these Southern skies, except it be the ship Argo, with Jason and the Argonauts, in search of the golden fleece. A condensed sketch of this wonderful journey we will give to our readers, so that they may realize the darkness of the days of Grecian mythology.

Colchis was the rock-bound shore of creation, against which the glorious orb of day dashed itself at every setting. Tubes not very unlike our conduit pipes, yet invisible, received the broken fragments of the sun, and carried them back to the Orient, where they were gathered together and became the blazing morning sun, riding high in the heavens another day, to be dashed to pieces against the eternal rocks of Colchis at night.

This is indeed a very easy method of solving the problem of day and night, and the hero that could navigate the unknown seas to Colchis, might well be promised a kingdom on his return.

The King of Thessaly—Anthamas—had two children, Phryxus and Helle. The step-mother of the son and daughter of Anthamas persecuted these childen, and in their flight for safety Murcury furnished them the Ram that grew the golden fleece. This Ram flew through the heavens in a journey to Colchis in modern balloon style, carrying on his back both Phryxus and Helle. In crossing the Dardenells, thereafter called Hellespont, Helle became dizzy and fell and was drowned. The Ram went on to Colchis, carrying Phryxus in his journey over the unknown seas, and in the end the Ram was slain as an offering to Jupiter, and his golden fleece given to Ætes, who ordered it to be kept in a consecrated grove at Colchis. Jason constructed the grandest ship of the age, and with a promise that he should be King of Thessaly on his return with the golden fleece, set sail with a few veteran volunteers for the land of the gods and the fleece of honor.

Tribulations met him at all points in his journey, birds that threw their feathers like porcupine quills, rocks that would not lie still and let him pass, and storms, and offended deities haunted him in his journey.

Jason at length reached Colchis, and King Ætes consented to let him take the fleece, provided that he would "yoke the two fire-breathing bulls of Vulcan to a plowshire of adamant, and plow with them four acres of land, consecrated to Mars, never before turned up. He was then to sow in the furrows the remaining serpent's teeth of Cadmus, now in possession of Ætes, and to kill the armed heroes which they produced, and at last to fight with and slay the dragon that guarded the the golden fleece."

Media loved Jason. Media was the daughter of Ætes. Juno and Minerva, goddesses, had instructed Media and she brought Jason through all right. He yoked the bulls, plowed the field, stupified the dragon, and sailed for Corinth and reached his destination with Media, his young and loving wife, and taking home with him the golden fleece.

Such is a condensed history of the ship Argo, and the Argonauts, as seen in the exalted teachings of Greek mythology; and then these valiant heroes and the gods sent this mighty ship up to the skies, and made it one of the Southern constellations.

If we now turn our attention homeward we shall pass the constellation of Argo, which, with ten bright suns, lies a little to our left and then on, a hundred trillion of miles, and we see a little speck as large as a cherry-stone—away far off, that is earth, the land of our nativity. Let us now take our telescope a moment and look at those bright stars that we see by natural vision. Look! the telescope brings to our view six thousand double stars, that to us had appeared as single. The polestar—Polaris—has an attendant star eighteen minutes off; and Rigel one only ten minutes off, appearing to us as only a single star.

Some 650 of these are, so to speak, tied together, and are called *physically united;* that is, they revolve around each other. Thus, Lyra is a binary star, while Orionis is a system of seven brilliant orbs.

These systems of stars have *periods* in which they perform entire revolutions around each other.

Ursa Major is a binary star; and since discovered, these suns have made one entire revolution around each other.

The periods in which eight of these double

stars have performed an entire revolution is very nearly one hundred years; while over three hundred have revolving periods of nearly a thousand years each. The orbits of these stars are immense. Thus sixty-one Cygnia is supposed to have an orbit of 5,028,771,000,000 miles in circumference. The stars we are passing are all aglow in the seven prismatic colors. Antares is red, Capello yellow, Lyra blue and Castor green.

But away yonder is the Solar System, supposed to embrace in its network of attractions one hundred and twenty-five planets, satellites and asteroids; the nearest one of these to the earth we inhabit is our faithful Luna—the Moon. Let us here stop a moment and look at its wonderful face. At some subsequent period, this orb appears to have been broken by volcanic forces, as the extinguished craters abundantly show, while at the present time no volcanic fires are visible. To us it shows a ragged exterior of mountains that are elevated from three to four miles, with little atmosphere and no verdure visible. But valleys and rocks appear in terrible confusion.

Revolving upon its axis consecutively every lunar month, obliges it to show the same face constantly to our telescopic observation; and so we must guess at the appearance of its other hemisphere.

We may now, if we choose, change cars, and take an express train of electricity, and arrive at our journey's end in eight minutes; having only 240,000 miles to travel, and we are at home.

But this world is not our long-abiding place— we *must* leave it. Still, may we not hope to secure to ourselves an unclouded title to those mansions, so bright and so glorious, on the other shore? And may both writer and reader, by and by, gain a happy admittance among the redeemed of the stellar skies, in the mansion and palace of God.

THE END.

www.ingramcontent.com/pod-product-compliance
Lightning Source LLC
Chambersburg PA
CBHW020123170426
43199CB00009B/614